GROUNDING
POLITICAL
DEVELOPMENT

◆

GROUNDING POLITICAL DEVELOPMENT

Stephen Chilton

Lynne Rienner Publishers ◆ Boulder and London

Published in the United States of America in 1991 by
Lynne Rienner Publishers, Inc.
1800 30th Street, Boulder, Colorado 80301

and in the United Kingdom by
Lynne Rienner Publishers, Inc.
3 Henrietta Street, Covent Garden, London WC2E 8LU

Library of Congress Cataloging-in-Publication Data
Chilton, Stephen.
    Grounding political development / by Stephen Chilton.
        p.   cm.
    Includes bibliographical references and index.
    ISBN 1-55587-172-0
1. Political culture—Philosophy. 2. Political development—Philosophy.
I. Title
JA75.7.C47   1990   90-27769
306.2—dc20   CIP

British Cataloguing in Publication Data
A Cataloguing in Publication record for this book
is available from the British Library.

Printed and bound in the United States of America

The paper used in this publication meets the requirements
of the American National Standard for Permanence of
Paper for Printed Library Materials Z39.48-1984.

Contents

Acknowledgments   vii

1 Introduction   1

2 The Analytical Method   11

3 Detailed Justification of the Five
   Fundamental Theoretical Requirements   23

4 Other Suggested
   Fundamental Theoretical Requirements   43

5 Two Recent Conceptions of
   Political Development   49

6 Defining Political Culture   57

7 Culture Is the Locus of Development   87

8 The "Ways of Relating" Perspective   95

9 The Political Practice of Genetic Epistemology   101

Bibliography   121

Index   129

About the Book and the Author   135

Acknowledgments

The nature of this work— the multiplicity of its issues and its concern with both exposition and defense—gives me the privilege of acknowledging a variety of friends and colleagues for a variety of contributions.

I am indebted to George Graham and Richard Kimber for their comments on Chapter 2, especially about the singularity or multiplicity of conceptualizations and about the relationship between normative commitments and conceptualizations. An earlier version of Chapter 4 was presented at the 1987 annual meeting of the American Political Science Association, at the roundtable "What Is Political Development?" I am indebted to Professors Robert Bates, James Caporaso, John Kress, Monte Palmer, Fred W. Riggs, Ezra N. Suleiman, and several anonymous reviewers for their encouragement and intelligent commentary. A shorter version of Chapter 6 appeared in the *Western Political Quarterly* 41, 3 (September 1988): 419–445; I gratefully acknowledge the *Quarterly*'s permission to use this material. An early version of this work was delivered at the 1986 annual meeting of the Midwest Political Science Association. Professors Leonard Champney, Lynn Deming, Stephen Douglas, Siegrun Fox, Craig Grau, John Kress, Beth Lau, Dean Mann, Richard Merritt, Lucian Pye, Steve Ropp, Manfred Wenner, Gadi Wolfsfeld, and several anonymous journal reviewers gave earlier incarnations of this chapter close, critical readings that sparked important improvements. My research into the conceptualization of political culture was supported in part by a grant from the College of Arts and Sciences Research Center, New Mexico State University, and in part by the hospitality of the Political Science Department, University of Illinois. An early version of Chapter 7 was presented at the panel, "Culture and Societal Development," at the 1989 annual meeting of the International Studies Association. This research was supported in part by a grant from the Office of International Education, University of Minnesota. I am indebted to Professors Tsuneo Akaha, John Kress, Han Park, and Yoshimitsu Takei for their comments. Eve Cole, Susan Coultrap-McQuin, Gerald Gaus, and Paul Sharp helped me think about Chapter 8. Earlier versions of Chapter 9 were presented at the 1988 annual meeting of the Southern Political Science Association and at the 1989 annual meeting of the Caucus for a New Political Science. I am indebted to Patricia Burns, Jonathan Casper, Harvey Jackins, Karl Magyar, John Martz, Patricia Morris, Monte Palmer, Han Park, David Smith, and three anonymous reviewers for encouragement and the expressions of doubt and confusion about genetic epistemology that inspired this work. A preliminary version of this chapter appears in *Studies in Comparative International Development* 25, 2 (Summer 1990):3–23.

My friends Craig Grau, Stephanie Hemphill, Don Kurtz, and Mara Sapon-Shevin maintained an attitude of relaxed confidence in and high expectations for me throughout the course of this work. As always, I deeply appreciate the professional assistance of Lynne Rienner and her friendly, competent staff. Of course, any remaining loose ends, confusions, and errors remain my responsibility, not that of the dear friends and colleagues listed above.

Stephen Chilton

1

Introduction

An earlier work of mine, *Defining Political Development* (Chilton, 1988b, henceforth termed *DPD*), advanced a new conceptualization of political development and also implied that other definitions were inadequate. Inexplicably, this blithe dismissal of the work of many previous scholars was met with caution instead of unrestrained praise. Many of my colleagues expressed objections to the work's argument and reservations about its implications.

I have gradually come to understand that, although the argument of *DPD* is basically self-contained, I left its philosophical underpinnings mostly to the reader's imagination. Because some logical elements are missing, or need elaboration, the power of the argument is to some extent concealed. Since the implications of the proposed framework are not drawn out, my colleagues are understandably reluctant to accept it wholesale. The image that occurs to me is of a structure suspended in space, with some of the internal beams and all of the supporting beams invisible. The objections raised against the structure arise from a natural wish to see that the beams really are present.

This book was written, therefore, to place *DPD* in its philosophical framework and to address the concerns that others have raised. In addition, its purpose is to elucidate the basic "ways of relating" orientation that informs the analysis presented in *DPD*.

This said, I turn to an overview of the argument of *DPD* and a preview of the concerns dealt with in the present work.

I. The Problem of Many Conceptions: The Analytical Method and Its Postulation of Five "Fundamental Theoretical Requirements"

A. *Flying Without a Pilot*

A curious characteristic of the field of political development is the absence of an agreed-upon conception of its core concept: political development itself. This confusion has existed for more than thirty years. The early, influential work of the Committee on Comparative Politics of the Social Science Research Council was funded by a Ford Foundation grant that stipulated, without further definition, that research was to be on "political development." The term is clearly analogous to economic development, but the disciplines of political science and economics are too different to make the analogy very helpful. Early definitions of the term thus had to be constructed without much guidance, and the inevitable confusion resulted. Over two decades ago, Lucian Pye (1966a:33) had already noted that "a situation of semantic confusion" surrounded this concept. He listed ten earlier definitions of the concept and proposed an eleventh definition that synthesized the themes of the ten others. Fred Riggs (1981) appended to his more recent analysis of the term a glossary of sixty-five different definitions offered in forty-nine different works by forty-one different authors (or joint authors). Still more recently, Han Park (1984:41–42, 54–55) listed thirteen different definitions (the majority of which neither Pye nor Riggs had mentioned) and offered his own definition as number fourteen.

This confusion has been perpetuated by the scant attention many "political development" works give to conceptualization. For example, despite its title, the recent *Understanding Political Development* (Weiner and Huntington, 1987) contains no index entry for the term,[1] even though the work begins with an acknowledgment of the variety of definitions of political development (p. xiii). Richard Bensel's *Sectionalism and American Political Development 1880–1980* (1984) discusses political development only in the sense of historical changes in the U.S. political system, i.e. political developments. (The terms "development" and "political development" appear neither in Bensel's index nor his table of contents.) Some articles with "political development" in their titles subsequently use the term not at all (e.g., Sollie, 1984; Dobelstein, 1985) or almost not at all (e.g., it is mentioned only once in Khalilzad, 1984–5, and Hope, 1985).

To some extent this confusion is inevitable and even desirable. Empirical researchers naturally tend to be impatient with conceptualization: their creative energy goes into inventing imaginative operational definitions and confronting the practical difficulties of measurement in the field, leaving little time for conceptualization; in any case, any political development researcher worth her[*] salt believes she already has a workable sense of what political development is. The behavioral tradition of political science can also lead researchers to believe that measurement procedures are more important substantively than abstract conceptions.[2] Finally, the political development concept's role as a "power word" (Riggs, 1981) creates further problems: the extra-academic advantages accruing to any one school's control over the term's meaning get mixed up with

---

[*]With the kind permission of the publisher, I use female pronouns throughout for the common gender. I find plural pronouns awkward to use, particularly in a work so concerned with distinguishing the isolated from the collective social actor; "he or she" and the like are awkward and intrusive; and alternation of gender requires the author to keep track of whether she is currently speaking of a female or male neuter. Since English currently possesses no gender-free personal pronouns, the choice lies between the masculine and the feminine. I hope the reader will welcome this opportunity to discover, from her own reaction to the consistent use of the female common gender, the connotations of the alternative usage.

intellectual discourse, making professional usage ideological as well as scientific. All in all, conceptualization gets short shrift.

As a consequence of these pressures, no general conceptual framework has emerged for studying political development.[3] As Huntington (1971) and Smith (1985) argue, results reported in the political development and modernization literature are neither comparable nor cumulative. While the field has generated subfields and "mid-range" theories,[4] it still does not possess an orienting conception of its own name.

B. Bail Out—or Learn to Fly?

This undeniable confusion has given rise to a conflict over the course researchers should adopt to deal with it. Some analysts—Fred W. Riggs and Samuel Huntington foremost among them—propose a straightforward abandonment of the political development concept.[5] Such analysts advance three strong arguments for their case. (1) Riggs argues that the term's status as a power word makes the term an "autonym"—a term having no clear referent or independent utility, but existing primarily as the focus of a struggle for power (or funding), and thus allowing no consensus on its definition. He asserts that once efforts to define the term are abandoned, "it becomes possible to sort out the many important and interesting variables or concepts that have clustered about the controversies over [its] meaning." To use the well-known formulation of Gallie (1956), political development may be an essentially contested concept. (2) Huntington does not go so far as to argue that the term has no meaning, but he does claim that the study of change offers as useful a focus for research as political development does, without the latter's conceptual difficulties. (3) Finally, beyond all theoretical arguments, there is simply the "enough is enough" argument: if after thirty years of intensive study we haven't been able to figure out what the concept means, perhaps we just ought to give up on it!

Three opposing arguments counter the above grounds for abandoning the search. (1) Confusion over the political development concept does not entail its inherent meaninglessness. Only in very special circumstances is it possible to prove the nonexistence of a concept.[6] The concept may exist but not yet be discovered, or the concept may already have been discovered, but analysts have not noticed the discovery, because they have either been wrapped up in their own research traditions or are uncertain how to recognize an adequate definition. The argument that political development is an "essentially contested" concept does not stand up; analysts confuse "contested" with "essentially contested," failing to recognize that Gallie (1956) demonstrated essential contestedness only under a set of assumptions that do not apply to political development. (2) While the study of change will certainly embrace the study of political development, the concept of development appears to be sharper than the concept of change. Intuitively, there would seem to be forces involved in development that are not present in other forms of change. If this is true, Huntington's (1971) proposal of a "change to change" would only obscure those special forces when what we really require is a sharper framework for handling them. This may explain why, despite all conflict and confusion over the concept, analysts persist in studying "development" instead of "change." (3) Finally, one can argue that while we cannot be happy about our thirty-plus years of confusion over the concept, our attempts to clarify it have themselves given rise to fruitful insights.[7] In any case, as noted earlier, it is possible that the lack of agreement arises from our own confusion rather than the absence of an adequate conception.

We seem to be on the horns of a rather nasty dilemma: either abandon the concept of political development, along with all its theoretical promise, or keep up the pursuit, with the risk of merely throwing good money after bad.

C.   The Analytical Method

In *DPD* I proposed to resolve this dilemma by using the following procedure. We first identify, in advance of any concept of political development, certain "fundamental theoretical requirements" (FTRs) that all theorists agree (or can be persuaded upon reflection to agree) a concept of political development should satisfy. For example, it seems obvious that a fully formed conception of development should state what it is, specifically, that changes in the course of development. This requirement, however modest it might seem, is not met by some previous conceptions, and so those conceptions must be ruled out of court. *DPD* argues that only its conception meets all five of the FTRs it advances. This procedure of identifying FTRs, eliminating conceptions inconsistent with them, and using them to develop a new, satisfactory conception, I call the "analytical method."[8]

Assuming a set of agreed-upon FTRs is found, we can then apply them to evaluate past, current, and future definitions. Note that since *all* FTRs must be satisfied before we are willing to call a concept "adequate," we are spared having to weigh the advantages of definition X against the different advantages of definition Y.[9]

This procedure has several advantages. First, it provides a systematic, agreed-upon procedure for evaluating alternative definitions, including future definitions, so that we will be able to *recognize* a good definition and distinguish it from less adequate ones. In the absence of FTRs, debates over alternative definitions become mired in unfocused, mutual criticism. Thus far, none of the alternative definitions has satisfied all the FTRs, a condition that may account for the confusion of the debates.

A second advantage of using FTRs to structure the discussion of alternative definitions is that agreement on the FTRs is relatively easy to achieve; I hope the reader will be persuaded, following the subsequent discussion, that theorists seem to have a common intuitive sense of how a concept of political development should behave, even if they don't yet have a universally acceptable description of it. Thus the analytical approach serves to *build consensus*.[10]

This process of analysis evaluates theoretical rather than operational definitions of political development. Our concern here is with conceptualizing, not operationalizing, and so we must apply the standards of systemic import, not the better-known standards of empirical import (Hempel, 1952:39–49). This is not to say that conceptualization can proceed independently of the discipline imposed by empirical results flowing from operational definitions; clearly, there is an interaction between the two. But we must guard against any limitations on our theoretical thinking imposed by what is readily measurable. Given the real scholarly pressures for immediate production of data, operationalization can easily swamp conceptualization, to the ultimate detriment of both. By insisting on *theoretical* requirements, the analytical method redresses that imbalance.

A number of concerns have been raised about this method. First, the logic of the analytical approach has not been accepted. One reader, for example, held that *DPD*'s tone of being a "geometric proof" was merely a rhetorical strategy. Since I indeed sought to provide an argument as irrefutable as a geometric proof, clearly my first task is to outline the logic that underlies my claim.

Other readers asked how the method would fare if there were several conceptions meeting all the FTRs. Even though this happy circumstance does not seem to have occurred in the case of political development, it is certainly a theoretical possibility, and a method unable to handle this circumstance would not be satisfactory.

Still other readers asked if the list of FTRs was complete, and if so, how one could prove it. If it were not, didn't that undercut the logic of the analytical method?

The analytical method employs only FTRs that have two characteristics: they must be dichotomous in nature, so that a conception either satisfies them or does not; and they must make only theoretical claims, that is, claims not depending on any empirical facts. These two "metacriteria" were both questioned by readers. Why should the FTRs be binary in nature? Why shouldn't they make empirical presuppositions of which we are confident? In effect, these questions ask whether the analytical method is the best method for theoretical work, even if it is logical as it stands. Why use the analytical method, when other approaches to conceptualization are able to make use of our theoretical knowledge and the careful weighing of differential advantages of alternative conceptions?

The nature of the analytical method, and replies to these questions, are presented in Chapter 2 ("The Analytical Method").

But beyond the general logic of the analytical method, questions were raised about its specific application to the concept of political development. Here there were two major concerns. First, some readers wanted more detailed justification of the five specific FTRs. They wanted further discussion particularly of "the micro–macro connection" and "normative justification." Chapter 3 ("Detailed Justification of the Five Fundamental Theoretical Requirements") addresses these concerns. Second, some readers suggested other FTRs, e.g., that the conception result in "laws" of development. Chapter 4 ("Other Suggested Fundamental Theoretical Requirements") discusses these suggestions.

II.   A New Conception of Political Development

The focus in *DPD* was not on the five FTRs but rather on a new conception of political development that was claimed to satisfy them. The interested reader should consult *DPD* for a full exposition of this conception, of course; for the sake of completeness I include here a brief description of the conception.

First, *DPD* simplifies its task by refusing to recognize ad hoc distinctions among economic, social, and political development, choosing instead to define development broadly and to let the natural cleavages of social-cognitive structure guide how we divide development into separate facets.

Second, *DPD* defines development in terms of certain changes in a culture, where the term "culture" is given an exact but idiosyncratic definition. Culture is defined "from the bottom up" as a way of relating shared by a group of people, the boundary of that group/culture being determined solely by that requirement of sharing. Thus cultures can overlap, according to how people use various ways of relating to coordinate their actions in various contexts. Cultures are not defined "top down" (i.e., by some external and thus problematic criterion like region or nationality), because such boundaries cannot ensure that the collectivity so designated shares anything in particular.

Third, this definition of culture yields an identity or correspondence between the way of relating shared in a given culture and the moral reasoning used to define and regulate that way of relating. Different ways of relating rely upon different systems of moral reasoning, which can in turn be divided among six different moral structures or stages. The existence of these stages has been established by a series of moral psychologists and genetic epistemologists (Jean Piaget, Lawrence Kohlberg, Carol Gilligan), even if some dispute remains about the exact nature of these stages.

Fourth and finally, development is defined as a shift of a culture from one way of relating to another that addresses and overcomes the structural ambiguities of its initial stage. One of the basic elements of the stage-structural view of moral reasoning is that every stage has inherent cognitive-structural ambiguities that constitute, psychologically, the "engines" or "motors" of development and, philosophically, the grounds on which each stage is normatively superior to its predecessor. (In the final stage, ambiguities are recognized and to that extent overcome in a permanent and ongoing dialectic.)

Taken all together, this definition of development is a powerful one. It is flexible, since the universality both of its definition of culture and of its view that moral reasoning underlies culture makes it applicable to all cultural traditions and to the connection between cultures and subcultures. It is sensitive to cultural nuance and adaptation, since its definition of culture and its recognition of the moral reasoning underlying culture can faithfully track the shifts of how people relate to one another. The definition is explicitly normatively grounded. This normative grounding is a source of constant attack, of course, but it makes the definition honest and corrigible. Finally, the definition's roots in both cognitive development and in the social construction of ways of relating provide a fertile source for plausible hypotheses about the dynamics of development.

III.   The Implicit Rejection of Previous Conceptions

DPD paid little attention to previous conceptions and implied that I rejected them. *DPD*'s final chapter did link its approach with certain conceptual traditions in political development,[11] but the work's discussion there and in Chapter 1 basically argued that previous conceptions either did not satisfy the FTRs or required special reinterpretation to do so.

However, this rejection of previous work was not made explicit, particularly in the case of recent conceptions, and some direct analysis of these conceptions is necessary. Such an analysis will also serve to show concretely how to employ the five political development FTRs. Accordingly, Chapter 5 applies the FTRs to two recent conceptions: those of Eckstein (1982) and of Park (1984). Readers interested primarily in political development and political culture, rather than in the intricacies of the analytical method or in the specific FTRs employed, should move directly to Chapter 5, returning to Chapters 2–4 as necessary. The present work is laid out so as to present the complete argument in as full detail as possible; readers satisfied with or indifferent to the argument's underlying logic can skip chapters as they please.

IV.   The Idiosyncratic Concept of Political Culture
in the Definition of Political Development

DPD defined political development in terms of specific types of changes in a political culture: changes that can be associated with changes in moral reasoning. In order to define political development in this way, however, the work had to advance its own conception of political culture. *DPD* explained this new conception only in a limited way, however, and did not justify its use. In Chapter 6 of the present work I look at the concept in more detail and explain why political culture *must* be defined in this way, quite apart from the happy circumstance that it allows a rational definition of political development.   Chapter 6 presents another example of the analytical method, in this case demonstrating its usefulness in the conceptualization of political culture.

Of course a cute new definition of political culture does not explain why political development must be defined as a change in culture instead of changes in some other concept. Chapter 7 explains why culture and no other concept must be the locus of development.

V.   "Ways of Relating" as a Focus

Both *DPD* and the present work flow from a "ways of relating" perspective, a perspective that indiscriminately lumps together social, economic, and political relationships. Such a broad view of human relationships would appear to have little "bite," but that turns out not to be the case. Viewing relationships generally enables us to bring normative issues to bear at all levels of human society, including the least well structured. This generality enables us to deal with, for example, feminist claims about the role and nature of hegemonic forces, forces that cannot be neatly labeled according to specifically social, economic, or political categories. Chapter 8 discusses how the "ways of relating" perspective bears on these issues.

VI.   The Definition in Terms of Moral Reasoning Development

DPD's idiosyncratic definition of political culture allows cultures to be ranked according to their level of moral reasoning development. The definition thus becomes linked both to an accurate system for scoring moral development stages (Colby and Kohlberg, 1987) and to a wealth of empirical information about moral reasoning development, generated by that system.

However, the use of Kohlberg's work (and the focus on moral reasoning development generally) raises a number of concerns. First, Kohlberg's work (like Piaget's) was invented by a Western, white, male, middle-class academic. How could a culturally universal theory of political development emerge from such work? Second, a related objection holds that Kohlberg's system improperly scores members of other cultures and genders. Third, critics fear that a cognitive-developmental perspective will provide an excuse for various forms of oppressive politics, perhaps giving rise to a meritocracy of moral reasoning, and/or to the dismissal of the interests of "low-stage reasoners." Finally, Kohlberg's theory was developed to apply to individuals, and Kohlberg himself specifically argued that it could not be used to evaluate societies as a whole. Chapter 9 discusses these objections and the implications of using the genetic-epistemological perspective.

Notes

1. The work gives no definition of political development. Subject index entries do appear for "development, definition of," "developmentalist model," and "development goals," but the last two references are not to definitions, and the first reference is to a simple definition of economic development as the growth in GNP per capita.

2. Hempel (1952: Section 7, esp. p. 31) explains why the extreme behavioralist position—that conceptualization has no role independent of operationalization—is too limited. Payne (1984:86–89) notes that the empirical study of development cannot substitute for its conceptualization.

3. Riggs (1967:337ff.) raises the question of whether the term political development denotes anything more than a general field of inquiry; if not, attempts at "definition" are

futile. He points out that the field of U.S. politics has established itself even though it possesses no single theory or unifying perspective. Granted, development studies are worthwhile even without a central term; nevertheless, most analysts seem to assume the existence of a unifying concept, and development studies would be greatly strengthened if the unifying concept hidden behind the current welter of approaches could be disclosed.

4. See, for example, the variety of theoretical approaches given in Weiner and Huntington (1987).

5. Huntington uses the term "modernization," not "political development." One of the confusions in this field is that some theorists discuss Westernization, some discuss modernization, still others discuss development, and some discuss change.

6. One way is to demonstrate a concept's inherent self-contradiction, as Bertrand Russell did for the concept of "the set of all sets," making use of the self-contradictory nature of the concept of "the set of all sets which are not members of themselves."

7. To take an example from another field, psychologists have found their battles over the concept "self" fruitful, even though no single concept seems to dominate. (I am indebted to Craig Grau for this observation.)

8. If philosophers have another name for it, I have been unable to discover it.

9. It could happen, of course, that different definitions meet a given FTR to different degrees, initiating a new debate. As will be seen below, the FTRs employed here are either satisfied or not; there are no "degrees" of satisfaction. I argue in Chapter 2 that every FTR will possess this dichotomous form.

10. In an ideal world, the ability of the challenges to end the debate over political development's meaning would be settled by an immediate, ringing endorsement (or lack of endorsement) of the challenges by all political development theorists. The situation is complicated, however, by researchers' natural tendency to forget their richest sense of political development as it becomes overlaid by their more immediate (and professionally crucial) concern to protect their own painfully constructed, once-acknowledgedly-partial-and-imperfect definitions. I believe that if the underlying challenges are actually stated, then development theorists will ultimately come around after they have had a chance to consider them. I recognize that this argument is also a perfect excuse for dismissing anyone's not "seeing the light," so it must be dealt with cautiously. But the possibility clearly exists that researchers might have reason to be wedded to their own formulation and might be reluctant to back up in order to reexamine foundational ambiguities. It is difficult to know whether researchers disagree over the meaning of the phrase because it is not in fact susceptible to a single definition, or whether, on the other hand, a unifying conception does exist, which, however, researchers do not immediately recognize because of pressures unrelated to theory. I am confident, though, that an open-minded discourse will inevitably bring the truth to light, whatever it may be. We can particularly look to the responses of development theorists who are not yet wedded to any particular definition.

11. Such theories include those of Hegel, Marx, and Pye, as well as theories of cultural progress and of cultural relativity.

2

The Analytical Method

I. The Problem of Social-Scientific Conceptualization

The basic task of social science theorists is to obtain *agreement* on *useful* conceptions. Thus our challenge is twofold. First, we need agreement on our conceptions in order to pursue truth in a sustained, cumulative manner. As Hobbes pointed out over three centuries ago, disagreement over the meaning of fundamental terms means a breakdown of discourse (Wolin, 1960: Chapter 8).[1] New conceptions are often proposed without eliminating their competitors. The long-term consequence is a welter of fundamentally different concepts, so that our research efforts, instead of adding one more grain of sand to the pile of knowledge, as the metaphor goes, only produce little dust balls scattered about our theoretical floor. In order to be truly helpful, a new conception must either eliminate previous conceptions or at the very least show how they are related to the "true" meaning, so that the little dust balls of knowledge can be swept together into something more substantial.

"Agreement" does not mean a unanimity of bald, unsupported opinion, however, because proposed conceptualizations cannot be held hostage to people who do not grasp the issues involved. Instead, agreement has to refer to the shared recognition or acknowledgment of good grounds for supporting a position. It must be based on a process of rational discourse rather than on one of competing stubbornness. In other words, we are in the position, made familiar to us by Habermas (1979a), of asserting absolute validity claims which we can only support contingently. Unanimity of opinion really pertains only to the ideal sphere of validity claims supported by good reasons; in practice, we are inevitably cast in the position of weighing people's agreement or disagreement against what we understand as their ability to grasp and formulate good reasons. The recursive nature of this process—that is, where we judge reasoners as well as reasons—reflects only our inability to reach an absolute truth.

Theoreticians have been sensitive to the need for agreement on the term "political development" and have consequently produced many theoretical critiques of previous conceptions of it, either in conjunction with a new conception or alone. Unfortunately, these critiques provide no positive direction. In some cases (e.g., Huntington, 1971; Riggs, 1981) they merely damn the entire

11

project of conceptualization without addressing the serious concerns that originally led to the proliferation of definitions. In some cases (e.g., Pye, 1966a) they synthesize existing definitions but do not clarify their unity. In some cases they do not provide systematic grounds for evaluating alternative conceptions, which might be broadly persuasive, but instead provide only little "advertisements" for their own conception.

But the achievement of conceptual agreement is not our only challenge, however difficult it may be. The second challenge is to find *fruitful* conceptions— conceptions whose theoretical insights produce empirical value. We want conceptualizations to flow naturally into theories that lay bare regularities of important social processes. The process of conceptualization thus passes beyond mere identification of specific variables to an implicit indication of what social processes exist, how they are related, and why they are important. In other words, a persuasive theoretical conceptualization should also be embedded in a fruitful theoretical framework. This requirement of theoretical fruitfulness is not opposed to that of theoretical agreement—presumably the fruitfulness of a theoretical framework will tend to bring agreement on the theoretical conceptions supporting it, and vice versa—but the two requirements are not prima facie identical.

We need to recognize and accept right away that a theoretically virtuous concept may not be easily operationalized. But in the long run it is our theoretical accuracy, not our operationalization, that carries us forward in great leaps.[2] I offer the analogous case of the medieval alchemists, another "pre-paradigmatic profession," whose unsystematic experiments led them to discover many interesting phenomena but who essentially marched in place until the great organizing framework of molecular theory enabled them to proceed systematically. The operational requirements of modern chemists (purity of ingredients, precision of temperature and proportions, etc.) are more exacting than those of the alchemists, but chemists' profit on this operational investment is enormous. So will it also be with the social sciences.[3]

Why is conceptualization so hard for the social sciences, particularly as compared to the physical sciences? We would seem to have every advantage. Physical science had to invent, almost from scratch, concepts of work, energy, power, force, momentum, acceleration, electron, molecule, and so on. Even concepts whose names existed previously (e.g., "work") took definitions having little to do with their former intuitive meaning. Because the physical world is not constructed by humans, we necessarily had to develop our conceptions of it "from the outside in." The social world, by contrast, is constructed by human beings, so we would expect social concepts to be obvious. Our language already has such socially central notions as power, legitimacy, the self, development, culture, prejudice, politics, and the like. Our intuitive understanding of these terms would seem to be all that is required for accurate conceptualizations. Why then do social science conceptualizations remain in such dispute?

Three forces seem to be at work. First, precisely because we approach social science from the inside, conceptualization is not taken very seriously. Since we "know" what culture is, for example, conceptual/analytical work is seen as theoretical nit-picking, taking time away from the "real" business of data gathering. As a result, conceptualization is pursued unsystematically. Methodology texts invariably consider issues of validity, but they do not discuss how useful and widely acceptable concepts can be reached in the first place. This is true even of methodological and philosophical works that directly consider the process of conceptualization. Hoover (1984), for example, jumps immediately from concepts to measurement, without consideration of how the concepts are created. Payne (1984) objects to the reification of terms like political development and modernization, opting instead to stick closely to operational definitions. Babbie (1986:98–102) distinguishes conceptualization from nominal and operational definitions, but then quotes Hempel (1952) in dismissal of conceptualization:

> A "real"definition, according to traditional logic, is not a stipulation determining the meaning of some expression but a statement of the "essential nature" or the "essential attributes" of some entity. The notion of essential nature, however, is so vague as to render this characterization useless for the purposes of rigorous inquiry (Hempel, 1952:6).[4]

Second, our conceptual problems also arise from various extratheoretical distortions of our theoretical discourse. For example, the reward structure of our disciplines currently favors empirical measurement over theoretical clarity. There is a proportionately strong pull to neglect theoretical accuracy in favor of creative operationalization and subsequent data gathering.[5]

Finally, disciplinary discourse is thrown into chaos by an absence of rigorous theorization and conceptual pruning. Social scientists justify their neglect of accurate conceptualization by holding to a "survival of the fittest" myth: that better conceptions will survive theoretical challenge, will produce better results, and will thus ultimately prevail. Researchers hold that their results are arbitrary relative to their operational definitions (or perhaps nominal definitions); or that definitions, while philosophically arbitrary, are disciplined only by their relative success in producing empirical findings. This attitude might be termed "conceptual pluralism."[6] The consequence of conceptual pluralism is the rise of competing conceptualizations, with much consequent theoretical and empirical confusion. Note, for example, the long history of research attempting to disentangle the concepts of "authoritarianism," "left" vs. "right authoritarianism," "conservatism," "ethnocentrism," and "prejudice." Note, to take an even more pertinent example, the long history of attempts to distinguish from one another "development," "modernization," "Westernization," and "change."

This definitional proliferation pollutes social science as a scientific enterprise. Proliferation may serve other functions—paying our salaries, letting us see our names in print, legitimizing the current regime—but it will not be science. One might argue that better conceptualizations will ultimately prevail, but this outcome is not inevitable: ease of measurement may outweigh theoretical rigor in determining career success. Even if this were not the case, the confusion attendant on such proliferation is clearly a terrible burden on the social-scientific enterprise.

II.   The Analytical Method

DPD addressed this problem of conceptual pluralism by using what it called the analytical method: a method for making decisive, rational choices among alternative conceptualizations. The analytical method makes the process of conceptualization systematic because it involves thinking clearly about fundamental theoretical requirements (FTRs) that the conception in question must meet, and then finding or inventing a conception that does so. If the FTRs have been well chosen, other analysts will agree with them and thus be forced, willy-nilly, into agreement with the conception the FTRs approve. If the FTRs have been well chosen, then the approved conception will have dug down into the heart of the social world, so that other conceptions will articulate smoothly with it in a unified, fruitful theory.

All of this puts great weight on the selection of the FTRs, of course, so from a logical standpoint we really haven't advanced very far: merely transferred the argument from a choice among conceptions to one among FTRs. However, it turns out that we are generally much clearer about what we want our conceptions to *do* (the FTRs) than we are about what they should *be* (the specific definitions). I think this will be clear from the examples of the FTRs for political development (in Chapter 3) and for political culture (in Chapter 6). At the end of the present chapter I discuss why the method appears to produce agreement and fruitful definitions.

After advancing and justifying its set of FTRs, the analytical method then makes both a narrow and a broad argument. The narrow argument is, "You *must* adopt this conception as against all other current conceptions, because it is the only one satisfying all the FTRs, which you yourself agree with."[7] The broad argument is, "You *should* adopt this conception because conceptions meeting the FTRs will be theoretically fruitful." The narrow argument is susceptible to direct, rational dispute. The broad argument, on the other hand, can be tested only indirectly through empirical research.

III.   Problems with and Attacks on the Analytical Method

Despite the straightforward logic of the analytical method, several questions are commonly raised about it. In this section I set forth these questions and reply to them.

A.   *Where Do the FTRs Come From?*

Must one resort to some infernal pact in order to get persuasive and fruitful FTRs? This important issue is raised by Russell Hanson (personal communication) and others, who hold my use of FTRs to be ad hoc, so that the method "produces plausible, but theoretically ungrounded results." I grant that I have no mechanical formula for discovering them, but I hope in the following discussion at least to demonstrate their human parentage.[8]

There are four major sources for FTRs. First are the elementary consider-ations of social science conceptualization. On the one hand, conceptions should be applicable across cultures; on the other hand, they should achieve this cross-cultural applicability in a manner that is sensitive to the uniqueness of each culture.[9] Conceptions should be operationalizable, at least in principle. Con-ceptions should be defined directly, not by reference to their causes, consequences, or correlates.[10] Complex conceptions should be defined as wholes, not as unstructured collections of constituent elements.

The second major source of FTRs is previous theoretical critiques. In the two areas I have investigated—development and culture—there is a wealth of critical work. Sometimes that work is in the service of new conceptions; sometimes it has a simple critical/destructive intent. In either case, the work advances legitimate concerns. Such concerns are particularly useful because they represent those FTRs that existing conceptions are having difficulty satisfying. It turns out, for example, that many of the critiques of Almond and Verba's (1963) conception of political culture identify precisely that point at which Almond and Verba's preoccupation with operationalization subverted Almond's (1956) earlier, better, theoretical formulation. Such critiques, in other words, mark points where theoreticians can easily lose their way.

The third major source of FTRs is the theoretical introductions to previous work in the field of concern. Almost every such work starts with a loose description of the concept in terms of the hopes the analyst places upon it. Even if the particular conception offered does not bear out these hopes (or fails to bear out hopes mentioned in other works), the hopes themselves are generally unexceptionable. Enshrining these common hopes as FTRs ensures that a conception satisfying them will both command agreement and reap the theoretical harvest that the many theorists have expected of it.

Finally, one can discover FTRs by noticing the theoretical characteristics of one's own preferred conception. I hope I will not be misunderstood here, for I decried above the practice of making FTRs into little advertisements of one's conception instead of generating basic, agreed-upon theoretical requirements. One cannot start with a pet conception and develop from it FTRs whose only reason for existence is to distinguish one's own from others' conceptions, because these FTRs will not command acceptance or will not have the air of penetrating to the heart of the issue. One's readers, set on guard by ad hoc, tendentious FTRs, will look skeptically at one's subsequent conception. How-ever, it is still legitimate, if risky, to develop a concept in interaction with its

FTRs, so that a thoughtful examination of one's theoretical intuition about the concept reveals plausible, important FTRs. I date my full conception of political culture from the summer afternoon when, after several weeks of digging through existing conceptions and critiques, and after getting a general sense of the conceptual approach I wanted to take, I sat back and asked myself why I felt mine was the correct conception. The resulting list of FTRs in turn helped me clarify my concept and articulate it more clearly. Thus, the difference between a true analytical method and the method of "little advertisements" is that one has to judge the FTRs on their own merits. The standard one does *not* apply is: will they distinguish my work from that of others? Instead, the standard must be: will the FTRs both command agreement and take us to the heart of social life?

This leads me to the issue of "metacriteria" for the FTRs. In my experience, FTRs invariably have two characteristics. First, they do not make any assumptions about the nature of empirical reality. For example, even though I believe wholeheartedly that Kohlberg's work on justice reasoning development is empirically correct, I don't embed it in my FTRs of political development. Not presuming empirical facts also means not excluding potentially uncomfortable facts. Thus in my discussion of political culture, one of the FTRs insists that conceptions of political culture not reduce culture to some lowest common denominator.

Although the absence of empirical assumptions is the goal, some FTRs will inevitably have to make certain basic assumptions like "Society exists," or "People will listen to each other's arguments to some extent," or "People are motivated to some degree by considerations of justice," and so on. Ultimately, the validity of the analytical method depends on the wide acceptability of these assumptions. The approach here is similar to that of John Rawls in his *A Theory of Justice,* where he gives his participants in the Original Position some sense that they are in a society, but provides them only facts that he believes everyone will recognize as relevant characteristics of the human condition.[11] Such empirical presumptions are always open to rational dispute, of course, but the ideal is that the FTRs should make as few and as obvious empirical presuppositions as possible.

A corollary of this is that the analytical method is most easily applied to concepts whose existence is generally acknowledged and widely applicable— to concepts, in other words, that do not belong exclusively to one theoretical framework or historical circumstance. This holds true, for example, for the concepts "political culture" and "political development" but not for "critical elections."[12]

A second metacriterion is that FTRs are either satisfied or not: there are no "degrees" of satisfaction. This dichotomous character is required by the logic of the analytical method; one argues that other conceptions *do not* satisfy all the FTRs, while one's own *does.* Requiring dichotomous FTRs also has the virtue of distinguishing theoretical from professional considerations.[13] For example, it would be a happy circumstance if our chosen conception could be easily operationalized, but "ease of operationalization" is not a legitimate FTR. One can easily conceive that proper and fruitful conceptions might be very difficult to operationalize, as they are in chemistry. Demanding dichotomous FTRs prompts one to advance only truly central FTRs—those one is willing to live or die by, theoretically speaking.

B. *How Do You Persuade Someone to Accept the FTRs in the First Place?*

The discussion so far has assumed that the FTRs command agreement, but clearly some analysts might not agree with one or more of them. How does one deal with this disagreement?

The analytical method is not a mechanical process for achieving Truth. There are no magic answers here; the FTRs have to carry their weight. The FTRs are human constructions and require thought and discussion before they command agreement. For example, in the next chapter I justify the five FTRs I used in defining political development. The arguments there range from the obvious to the complex.

Remember, however, that with an adequate number of FTRs, one's argument does not hinge on any one of them. Typically, alternative conceptions will violate several of the FTRs. Unless the disagreeing analyst takes issue with all those FTRs, she will still be forced to accept the one surviving conception. One need not get wrapped up in disputing every disagreement. [14]

But doesn't this possibility of disagreement overthrow the whole logic of the analytical method? After all, if the analytical method merely shifts the debate from the level of conceptions to the level of FTRs, disputes at the one level will simply be translated into the other. If the FTRs are themselves subject to dispute, what does the analytical method gain us?

First, one can often achieve remarkable results with a few obvious FTRs: close examination of the many proposed conceptions of political development and political culture reveals that most of them are dismissed even by the simplest of theoretical considerations. However, this answer is not fully satisfactory. Such successes are short lived, because they depend on earlier theorists having failed to be very precise in their conceptualizations and thus having violated the most obvious of FTRs. If those conceptualizations were to be tightened up, however, the disputes would be renewed over more controversial FTRs. An example will make this plain: Many development theorists define development in terms of its consequences instead of directly. Their conceptions are certainly inadequate on that basis, but it is clear that they may well have a conception of development per se and are only referring to its consequences as a shorthand (or as a lapse of theoretical rigor). If they redefined their conception of development more directly, the result might not be dismissed as easily. Although the analytical method forces theorists to avoid sloppy conceptualizing, it is not a magic way for simple FTRs to resolve fundamental debates.

The virtue of the analytical method really arises from the interplay it forces between theoretical considerations and particular conceptions. In essence, it brings an additional source of light to bear on the problem of conceptualization. Rather than being condemned to direct clashes between conceptions, we can also employ our theoretical sensibilities. The analytical method makes explicit the process of theoretical discourse. The theoretical considerations embodied in FTRs have always played a part in theoretical discourse about conceptions, but they can be lost from one dispute to the next. Enshrining them as FTRs makes them more readily applicable to new disputes and allows them to be the subject of direct discussion themselves, thus establishing a new and potentially enlightening level of discourse.

C. *How Many FTRs Should There Be, and How Do We Know We Have All of Them?*

The "narrow" logic of the analytical method only requires as many FTRs as necessary to exclude all but one candidate conception. But there are good reasons to develop as many FTRs as possible. First, the more FTRs employed, the more persuasive one's argument becomes. People may dispute the validity of certain FTRs, and if the argument hinges on all of them, it fails to persuade. Using numerous FTRs may be theoretical "overkill," but it is better to have five too many FTRs than one too few. Moreover, the more FTRs employed, the more confidence we have that the surviving conception will continue to survive. A minimal number of FTRs leads to the suspicion that FTRs may lurk in the wings that would exclude the surviving conception.[15] Finally, the more numerous and varied the FTRs, the more confidence we have of the theoretical fruitfulness of any surviving conception.

It is impossible to know when one has all the FTRs. In fact, it seems plausible that any reasonable conception could have an infinite number of FTRs. The issue will always be what criteria people are able to agree on, and this list may increase indefinitely as our theoretical acumen increases.

D. *What if People Advance Their Own FTRs to Invalidate Your Own Conception?*

The analytical method is not a party attended by invitation only. Others are free not only to criticize existing FTRs but also to propose their own—presumably in the service of their own conceptions but in any case not necessarily in the service of your own pet conception. How are you to deal with such challenges?

It should be obvious that you have to deal with others' challenges in the same way you are asking them to deal with yours. You must examine each proposed FTR to see if you agree with it. (The "metacriteria" discussed above will be helpful in this evaluation.) If, upon inspection, you can find no fault with a new FTR, you have no choice but to bite the bullet and accept whatever logical consequences follow from it.

E. *What if NO Conception Meets the FTRs?*

It is conceivable, particularly as the list of FTRs expands, that all existing conceptions might be eliminated. This does not invalidate the analytical method. Two responses are called for. First, reexamine the list of FTRs to discover whether they are inconsistent—that is, self-contradictory. If they are, this indicates either some error in your list of FTRs or else the basic irrationality of the conceptual enterprise on which you have embarked. Recognition of an inconsistency among the FTRs will prompt either revision of some of them or development of an important "impossibility theorem."[16]

If the FTRs are not obviously inconsistent, then you must develop your own conception. Once more, I caution that there are no magic solutions to the problem of conceptualization. Presumably a new, satisfactory conception will emerge from careful inspection of previous concepts, of the FTRs, and of the points of conflict between the two.

F. *What if Someone Proposes Another Conception Satisfying the FTRs?*

If faced with multiple concepts, you first need to check that other conceptions do indeed satisfy all the FTRs. Like most people, analysts can fall prey to wishful thinking: "My own conception is wonderful, so I don't need to look very closely at the FTRs."[17]

But assume the alternative conception does satisfy all the FTRs. This is not at all destructive of the logic of the analytical method but rather a wonderful opportunity for theoretical discourse about the relative merits of the two conceptions. As I said earlier, the analytical method is not a machine for grinding out Truth. The process of conceptual development through the analytical method is a process of reflective equilibrium (Rawls, 1971), where FTRs and conceptions discipline one another, advancing both the theoretical sensibility that produces the FTRs and the conception favored by them.

IV.   One Conceptualization or Many?

The analytical method takes the "unitary" position that the central concepts of social science ultimately have only one perfect conceptualization. Obviously this metatheoretical assumption cannot be proven, but responses to earlier versions of these arguments indicate that it requires some discussion.

The term "central concepts" needs explanation. Here again, I find Rawls's image of the Original Position to be of great use: concepts are central only if we would admit them behind the Veil of Ignorance. Concepts like "culture" or "development" refer to existential conditions of human life, so that we lose no generality of result by admitting knowledge of them into the Original Position. They constitute part of what I imagine Rawls (1971:137) means by "the general facts about human society, . . political affairs [, and] the basis of social organization."

I am not concerned about the uniqueness of conceptualizations of more peripheral concepts, for two reasons: (a) their conceptualization may well vary; and (b) they may not be fruitful. The concept "party identification," for example, is unique to a particular social formation, having neither cross-cultural applicability nor broad normative implications. Different political frameworks will command different conceptualizations of the term, and there seem to be no transcendental grounds for preferring any one of the term's different usages. In many political frameworks the term may have no meaning at all. The analytical method may help clarify meanings in such cases, but it may also run up against an "essentially contested concept."

Furthermore, even if agreed upon, peripheral concepts may not be fruitful. Given that they do not strike to the heart of human experience, the theories in which they play a part will necessarily be contingent, limited, or uninteresting. Much of the rational choice literature strikes me this way.

But let us return to the issue of the "unitary" position. Even for central concepts, why assume only one perfect conception? Here the best answer I can give is that the alternative has the most unfortunate consequences. To assume that fundamental aspects of human life have multiple conceptualizations—not just empirically, in the sense that people factually do disagree, but rather theoretically, in the sense that they can never come to agreement—means an abandonment of communicative action itself. It means that people cannot, never will, and need not even try to discuss their different experiences and perspectives with one another. It means they are opaque to one another—that the differences in their perspectives not only exist but are also forever unbridgeable. In short, "conceptual pluralism" ultimately represents not a respect for others' positions but instead a resigned ignorance (if not an outright dismissal) of them. Under such an assumption, rational discourse becomes merely strategic action, arguments merely contests of wills, and societies merely battlegrounds.

But the metatheoretical assumption of a single, "right" conceptualization should not be confused with the contingent, theoretical claim that a specific formulation is the only one possible. The "unitary" position looks totalitarian when compared to the "conceptual pluralist" position. In fact, the exact reverse is the case: the "conceptual pluralist" position, by denying the possibility of rational discourse, leaves us only the totalitarian means of force and deception as mechanisms for producing theoretical agreement, while the "unitary" position requires us only to keep honest discourse alive.[18]

Notes

1. The current Towers of Babel erected on the sites of "culture" and "development" are evidence of this problem. Note the consequent attempt by Huntington (1971) to abandon the concept of development and by Riggs (1981) to deny its very existence.
2. Dowding and Kimber (1983) take this position with respect to political stability.

See also Lehman (1972:362) with respect to political culture.

3. Our position is analogous to the alchemists' in still another way. Alchemy was dominated not by the search for truth itself but by certain specific desires, like the desire to change base metals into gold—an enterprise that could be financed by wealthy patrons. As long as those specific desires were the goal, no systematic knowledge could be obtained. We now do in fact have methods by which base metals can be changed into gold, but these methods would almost certainly not have been discovered by alchemic progress. Like alchemy, social science finds itself dominated by the quest for social control. Its new patrons are primarily the representatives of the established order, whose interest does not lie in the discovery of truth but in the management and control of particular social problems. As long as social science sacrifices the search for truth to the search for social control, truth will elude it.

4. To be fair to Hempel, however, his subsequent discussion of "explication" (1952:10–12, following Carnap, 1950, Chapter 1) does contemplate conceptualization beyond the mere linguistic analysis of conventional usage:

> The considerations leading to the precise definitions are guided initially by reference to customary scientific or conversational usage; but eventually the issues which call for clarification become so subtle that a study of prevailing usage can no longer shed any light upon them. Hence, the assignment of precise meanings to the terms under explication becomes a matter of judicious synthesis, or rational reconstruction, rather than of merely descriptive analysis: An explication sentence does not simply exhibit the commonly accepted meaning of the expression under study but rather proposes a specified new and precise meaning for it (Hempel, 1952:11).

5. I believe, but do not here insist, that value-laden concepts like political development are particularly prone to distortions arising from hegemonic control of theoretical discourse. Control of this kind is currently exerted along lines of class, occupation, gender, ethnicity, nationality, and so on. One need not presume conspiracy or ill will to recognize that definitions of development advanced in a milieu consisting primarily of white, male, and middle-class intellectuals, educated almost exclusively in the United States, may lack a certain breadth of perspective.

6. Conceptual pluralism also arises from the pleasant but scientifically unfortunate *politesse* that prevails among social scientists. The murky nature of social science has over time rewarded its students more for their tolerance of others' ridiculous ideas than for their scientific accomplishments in refusing to put up with nonsense.

7. This argument combines three claims: (1) "For each FTR, only conceptions meeting its requirements are acceptable"; (2) "The proposed conception meets all the FTRs"; (3) "No other existing conception meets all the FTRs." There is an implicit fourth claim, which I will discuss later, to the effect that there are no universally acceptable FTRs that the proposed conception would not satisfy.

8. But see the discussion of "metacriteria" below.

9. These desiderata apply to conceptions that we consider foundational to social science—conceptions that are "always already," as Habermas has it, part of the fabric of social life. Conceptions of development and of culture would seem to be such concepts; it is difficult to conceive of social life at all without them. Conceptions of "clan" or "marriage," by contrast, are temporary, contingent social constructs, and so might be readily conceptualized by means other than the analytical method described here.

10. Of course such causes, consequences, and correlates might be employed to measure them, with the usual considerations of validity and reliability.

11. The fact that many people object to Rawls's theory on the grounds that *more* facts should be adduced is irrelevant here.

12. Of course the analytical method can still be employed within a given framework to command agreement among that framework's adherents. My feeling is, however, that

its success in resolving disputes will be much less, because the concept's narrow focus gives less theoretical purchase.

13. This discussion recalls Kant's distinction between hypothetical and categorical imperatives. Hypothetical imperatives are derived from the desire to achieve some nonuniversal goal, while categorical imperatives are derived from the conditions of thought itself.

14. It does happen, however, that analysts use the perceived inadequacy of one of the FTRs to dismiss an entire argument. These attacks are only of tactical concern, however; such illogical arguments do not dent one's conclusions.

15. I will not dwell on the ad hominem suspicion that the analyst has deliberately stopped looking for other FTRs for fear that they might upset her theoretical apple cart.

16. A well-known example of such an impossibility theorem is Arrow's (1951) paradox, showing that no social welfare function exists that satisfies five plausible FTRs.

17. Of course, an analyst proposing another conception may not abandon it even if you demonstrate that it violates some of the FTRs. As always, she can challenge those FTRs themselves.

18. For example, Chapter 6 makes the contingent claim that its conceptualization of political culture is the only one satisfying the nine FTRs of that concept. The claim is expressed absolutely, and some readers have taken it as making a claim beyond argument. But the reverse is true: its claim about political culture is inherently relativized by the grounds on which it is made: its satisfaction of the FTRs. By the very terms of its argument it lays itself open to continued discourse about its validity.

3

Detailed Justification
of the Five Fundamental
Theoretical Requirements

Several readers of *DPD* have asked for a more detailed explanation of the five fundamental theoretical requirements, saying that the FTRs are not as obvious or as widely acceptable as claimed. These readers are particularly concerned with the two FTRs of normative grounding and the micro–macro connection. This chapter addresses these concerns, describing and justifying the five current FTRs, especially the two controversial ones. The first three of the FTRs follow from basic considerations of scientific conceptualization; the final two from more complex considerations.

I. Locus of Development

The term development implies that something changes. Development therefore has to be a change in some *thing*. This is the brunt of the "locus of development" FTR: that the analyst specify clearly what it is that changes. It is not enough to point to a general sense that "things" are changing, as if one has seen some flicker of movement but not the thing moving. Studying the physiology of development requires commensurate knowledge of its anatomy.

General terms like "society" or "politics itself" (Eckstein, 1982) do not delimit clearly what the domain of our theoretical attention should be. "A society," for example, could be a single hamlet or the entire world; the term leaves unclear how we delimit our attention. We can also imagine one part of "society" developing independently of another, which suggests that we can profitably make a more exact demarcation of development.

The need for focus arises from our sense that different foci result in quite different theories of the developmental process itself. We could study the development of the universe as a whole, but our studies would not be particularly useful in understanding the development of a state. When we lose the boundaries of development, we lose a sense of whatever uniqueness and integrity the process has.

DPD addresses the "locus of development" FTR by defining development as a change in a culture, where culture has a specific demarcation. (See Chapter 6 in this book; *DPD*'s definition of culture appears in its Chapter 2.)

II. Recognition of Development

We also need to be able to recognize development when it occurs, either by specifying the developmental sequence directly (e.g., naming the continuum; describing a sequence of states) or by positing a developmental criterion (e.g., complexity). As Huntington (1971) argues in his attempt to discard the study of development, development without a means of identifying it cannot be distinguished from any arbitrary change.[1]

I originally termed this FTR the "nature of development," but I have come to recognize that we may not be able to name exact states in advance. The difficulty here arises from the problem of whether development is properly conceived of as teleological or experimental in nature, a distinction that appears in biology between the development of an organism and the development of a species. The teleological development of an organism means the expression of the properties wired into it. The organism changes, but along a track predictable in advance. A species, on the other hand, does not develop as an entity. Instead, a certain portion of an existing species breaks with its fellows on the basis of new genes. This sort of development is not the unfolding of a predetermined pattern but an experiment, hopefully an adaptive one.

Is political development teleological or experimental? Both senses are used in political discourse, but only the latter sense seems appropriate to the study of political development. The former sense is used when we refer to political developments, plural, implying that one set of circumstances has naturally unfolded into the new set of circumstances. Circumstances of which we were formerly unaware may have come into view, but we continue to believe, at least retrospectively, that we are still observing the same sort of game.[2] The sense of development as an experiment, however, would seem to be more appropriate for the field of political development, which concerns itself with basic "ruptures" in existing social games. When true development occurs, we are able to look back and recognize a fundamental change in the rules.

The case for regarding development as experimental instead of teleological will grow stronger when, in a later section, I argue that development must be normatively grounded. Teleological development is not susceptible to normative evaluation, while experimental development is.[3] For all these reasons, the FTR is thus better termed "recognition of development."

DPD addresses the "recognition of development" FTR by looking at the cognitive structure of each culture. A culture whose underlying cognitive structure becomes more integrated and comprehensive than before (resolves existing ambiguities in how people are to relate to one another) is recognized as having become more developed.

III. Exact Specification

Theorists need to define development directly—i.e., to define development *itself*—instead of defining it only in terms of its causes, consequences, correlates, and constituent elements. Here I am not objecting to our pressing beyond development itself to these associated aspects of it, but rather to our thinking that such indirect references constitute a definition. When the distinction between direct and indirect definitions is stated thus baldly, it is apparent that definitions should be direct. Even if this were unclear as an abstract proposition, it is clear from our practical concerns with development. We find that direct definitions of development are more helpful than indirect ones in understanding developmental dynamics and thus in fostering development. This is most obvious in the case of consequences and correlates. It may be that development results in air pollution or is correlated with air pollution, but knowing this helps us neither understand development nor produce it.

A somewhat harder case is that of definitions of development in terms of causes. Surely our ambitions are served more directly by understanding development's causes than by defining it. Unfortunately, several problems make such a focus on causes less useful than direct definitions of development. First, many causes are not directly manipulable. Religious movements may create development, but they cannot be summoned up on command. Second, many causes are not conscionable. Even if we were able to create civil war, or a plague, or a social class's "loss of status respect" (Hagen, 1962), our conscience would not permit it. Third, causes themselves are contingent on many conditions, including the action of the development agents themselves. Causes that are efficacious in one historical period may not be in another.[4] Causes that work when they happen autonomously may go astray when they are applied by design. For example, suppose enormous, sudden population loss caused development; U.S. nuclear destruction of half a country would probably have rather different effects!   Fourth, and probably most important, FTRs should not assume empirical facts. (I discussed this in the previous chapter.) Definitions of development in terms of causes assume that the causal link will remain stable over time and circumstance, a proposition that can only be empirically defended if we have a theoretically prior, direct definition of development.

Finally, development should not be defined in terms of one of its constituent parts, or even in terms of all of them. Granted, development has numerous constituent parts of no obvious integration: it seems to involve changes in law, in individual psychology, in institutional patterns, in historical memory, in popular culture, in birth rates, and so on.[5] This variety makes it hard to conceptualize. Some people hold that development's multifaceted nature makes this FTR impossible to satisfy and thus theoretically useless; they would suggest that definitions in terms of the many facets should be permitted. The difficulty with this view is that a multifaceted conception of development does not wring as much information from our analyses as we would like. Pye's (1966a) well-known "syndrome" definition of development—whatever its merits otherwise—does not explain why the three facets of development (equality, capacity, and differentiation) occur together in the development process. If they do not, then development becomes only an index score of otherwise unrelated phenomena, a conception to which we may be driven, but one from which it is unhelpful to start. To take a biological example, a definition of someone's development in terms of increasing height plus increasing weight plus an increasing number of neurons, etc., would allow us to miss the fact that these changes are integrated with one another in very precise ways. A complete understanding of development would include an understanding of the connection among development's facets, not just a list of them.

DPD addresses this FTR simply by defining development itself. Discussions of development's causes, consequences, correlates, and/or constituents are always subordinated to the direct definition.

IV. The Micro–Macro Connection

Development must be defined to embrace both the micro level of individual behavior and the macro level of social institutions. Neither individual-centered nor institution-centered definitions can be satisfactory alone. One argument for this claim is, of course, the vast literature on development written from each of these two perspectives. Institutional capacity, legal infrastructure, party systems, and parliamentary institutions—as well as many other macro-level phenomena— have been cited at one time or another as bound up in development. At the same time, development has been attributed at least as often to the various micro-level considerations embodied in people's beliefs, attitudes, and values: culture, partisanship, public-regardingness, and so on. The degree of theoretical interest in both the micro and macro levels in development would suggest that it involves both levels.

This is not a decisive argument, however. It could be that one side (i.e., the micro or macro side) is mistaking some cause (or consequence, or correlate) of development for development itself. If that were the case, then development would "really" lie with the other side. The FTR of exact specification requires that this possibility be addressed.

There is a more telling argument, however, for insisting that a definition must embrace both the micro and macro levels: the argument I advanced in *DPD* (pp. 9–10). Basically, the argument has the form of a proof by contradiction. First, I show that development cannot be defined in terms of changes solely at the micro level. A moment's thought shows that a situation in which more-developed people (in whatever sense) interact through *exactly* the same institutions would not be considered development; the continuation of older, more venal ways of relating would brand their polity an underdeveloped one, contradicting the assumption that we have adequately defined development solely in micro terms. Second, I show on the other hand that development cannot be defined solely at the macro level. Since developed institutions cannot exist without people capable of sustaining them, we would not consider developed a polity in which "developed" institutions were imposed on people unwilling or unable to operate them properly. (Here I have in mind particularly U.S. attempts to impose its vision of government on the Vietnamese.) This contradicts our assumption that we have adequately defined development solely in macro terms. It follows, then, that development cannot be defined solely in terms of either micro-level or macro-level considerations, and thus any adequate conception of development must incorporate an understanding of how the two levels are related to each other in the course of development.

DPD addresses this FTR by defining development in terms of changes in culture. Because culture must be publicly common, change in culture means not just a change in individual capacity to employ cultural ways of relating but also a change in the actual use of these ways. This location of culture as intermediate between individuals and institutions is discussed further in Chapter 7.

V.   Normative Grounding

The last and most controversial of the FTRs holds that our conception of development must be normatively grounded, so that when a polity (or whatever locus we finally settle on) develops, the new state is morally preferable to the old. "Morally preferable" is here used in a strong sense of preferable according to universal criteria of moral judgment, not in the weak sense of merely conforming to one person's or group's conception of morality.

Given the profound debates over normative evaluation of social systems, this requirement would seem to sink all hope of obtaining any definition of development.[6] Nevertheless, there are important philosophical reasons for insisting on this FTR. Difficulty in satisfying it is no excuse for ignoring these reasons. (In any case I believe it can be satisfied.) Let us look at these reasons in detail.

The argument is in two parts: first, that any complete theory of social change (thus including any complete theory of development) has to incorporate a normatively grounded theory of moral choice; and second, that a conceptualization of development has to align itself with those normative grounds. The first argument hinges on the observation that people are free to act, and in fact sometimes do act, on the basis of moral concerns that are quite distinct from other causal pressures upon them. This freedom to act means that a *complete* theory of social action must incorporate a theory of their moral judgment. However, because such theorizing is itself potentially a cause of social action, the theory must hold reflexively, that is, people's knowledge of the theory must not affect their adherence to the behavior predicted by that theory. The only such theory is a normatively grounded one, so that the role of moral behavior in the theory is one that the actors themselves would be willing to endorse.[7]

Our reluctance to define development in normative terms stems not from our settled conviction that development is *not* normative but rather from our reluctance to deal with the thorny issues that normative discourse inevitably raises. Our experience in Vietnam (and the underlying imperialistic moralism from which adventures like that continue to flow) gave us good reason to fear normatively involved theory and to suspect its impartiality. But once we agree that any complete theory of social change *must* deal with the problem of normative grounding, the major objection to defining "development" in normative terms disappears. To understand society we have to grasp normative issues—or so I will argue below—and thus we can give renewed credence to our intuitive sense of development as normative improvement.

The remainder of this chapter, then, is devoted to proving the more difficult part of my claim, namely, that any complete theory of social change (that is, change of any form, whether "developmental" or not) must inevitably incorporate a normatively grounded theory of social choice.

A.   Introduction

To what extent, or in what way, do we[8] need to pay attention to normative considerations when constructing theories of social change?[9] Three distinct positions are possible. The first form of social change theory does not rely on or incorporate normative considerations in any way. In such theories people act out of necessity or under compulsion: without choice. The forces underlying social action may be historical, psychological, or technological, but they are not normative. Such *i*mpersonal theories of social change I will here term change/i theories.

Change/i theories may be represented by Lynn White's classic *Medieval Technology and Social Change* (1962), which sees social change as arising from technological discoveries like the stirrup and the plough.[10] The stirrup, for example, made possible the use of force in ways not possible earlier in history, enabling certain people—the possessors of the technology—to insist more easily on their own way of relating, inducing acquiescence through the threat of force.   The new technology constrained not just the unmounted peasant, however; it also constrained the mounted warrior himself to live in certain ways (White, 1962:28ff.). In White's view, social change comes about not through the imposition of one group's moral preferences on another but instead through technology's broad, unanticipated impact on all groups. Theories of technology-induced change are impersonal in their research focus, even if we retrospectively (and irrelevantly) evaluate these changes morally.

The second form of social change theory admits that normative choices by social actors affect social change to some degree, but explains away these choices by means of some theory of normative choice resting on nonmoral factors. This empirical theory is not itself normative in character, since its purpose is not to make any normative claims about actors' choices but only to predict or explain them. The prediction or explanation may be made on the basis of non-normative causes;[11] in any case the normativeness of the cause is not seen as germane. Theories of social change incorporating such an *e*mpirical theory of normative considerations I will here term change/e theories.

Change/e theories include any economic determinism or "vulgar" Marxism that sees social change as arising in part from philosophical, religious, or moral doctrines, but that also sees adherence to such doctrines (as well as their origins) as flowing not from the inherent validity of the doctrines themselves but rather from their adherents' location in the class structure (and, behind that, from the mode of production creating such a class structure). In this theory normative considerations play a role in social change, but they appear only as derivatives of non-normative considerations.[12]

A non-Marxian example of a change/e theory is L.T. Hobhouse's *Morals in Evolution: A Study in Comparative Ethics* (1906). Hobhouse surveys the moral codes of many civilizations and finds a steady advancement in moral values.[13] He explains this advancement, however, only in terms of a conjectured "survival of the morally fittest," in much the same manner as Edmund Wilson (1975) explains altruism in terms of its survival value for the altruist's genetic code. Ultimately, that is, Hobhouse explains morality not in its own terms but as a consequence of the non-normative physical and biological forces that determine survival.

The third form of social change theory includes, like change/e theories, an embedded theory of normative choice, with the additional proviso that the embedded theory is normatively grounded—that is, its causal explanations involve to some degree the nature of morality itself. Morality is here taken to be a domain sui generis, so that normative considerations can only be explained in their own terms, not as deriving from some non-normative domain. Such normatively grounded theories of social choice I will here term change/n theories.[14]

I am aware of only two examples of change/n theories: *DPD* and Radding (1985). Space limitations prevent an exposition here of the complex arguments involved; I will discuss them briefly later.

The burden of my argument is that only change/n theories are theoretically satisfactory.

B.   *Social Institutions Are Based on Ways of Relating*

Meaningful social intercourse (the Weberian–Parsonian "action") depends upon the participants sharing a common framework for interaction—a "way of relating." Such a framework creates meaning by structuring behavior, so that mere physical motion acquires an intellectual status through its location in a context common to all parties. When, encountering Al in a back alley, Bob produces a gun, Al and Bob immediately share a common understanding of the situation, despite the differing roles they happen to play in it. Their interaction is meaningful, if unpleasant; actions and reactions stand in definite relation to one another and are thus imbued with meanings one could not deduce from the physical motions alone.[15]

Such frameworks of meaning often go unnoticed, because in stable social systems people already share them with their associates. When I arrive in my classroom I don't have to explain to my students how I expect to interact with them; we already share that framework. Only rarely do people experience the role conflicts that require a real decision among alternative ways of relating.

The phrase "ways of relating" tends to raise images of family rituals, classrooms, or specific pair relations—the small frame, involving a few people knowing one another well. Such images are too limited, however. Laws, legal systems, governments, states—all represent ways of relating shared among millions of people. The neighbor who just asked to borrow my car relates to me in a way that comprehends laws about car theft, liability, and so on. Even though our knowledge of each other is only casual, our interactions are nonetheless guided by definite understandings.

Social action involves, then, a coordinated choice by a set of actors among alternative ways of relating and a subsequent choice of behavior appropriate within the way of relating that has now become normative.[16] Note again that meaningful action requires coordination among actors; all must acquiesce in the framework in order for behavior to have social meaning. But only acquiescence, not support, is required to establish a way of relating as the norm. No assumption is made of a "value consensus" or of an agreed-upon "social contract"—only of a common acquiescence.[17]

The choice among ways of relating is, of course, the choice of interest in political change studies. Political change is not the mere change of actors, with the basic way of relating remaining the same, but a structural political change. Structural political change occurs when people relate to one another through a new set of social categories not homomorphic to categories obtaining previously. The requirement of nonhomomorphism eliminates superficial, cosmetic changes such as new titles disguising old positions or new personnel maintaining old power relationships.[18] In structural change, old relationships disappear, displaced or reconfigured by new ways of relating. The linguistic structure of political discourse changes (Foley,1986).[19] It is with such structural changes, not with superficial or cosmetic ones, that this article deals.

C.   It Follows from B that Theories of Social Dynamics Require an Embedded Empirical Theory of How People Choose Among Ways of Relating

Even though every social change arises through people's *choice* of what ways of relating to adopt, the importance to society of such choice is often obscured. Many of our actions are made in the face of reasons so obvious that to notice them at all seems odd. For example, most people would probably require some time to construct an explanation of why they automatically "choose" to pay their restaurant tab. Even in situations where people do think of themselves as really "choosing," choice arises only within a taken-for-granted structure of alternatives and considerations. To grade an essay A- or B+; to vote Republican or Democratic; to eat at Wendy's or Burger King—none of these choices changes the system of social categories within which the choices appear. Such choices may interest us as the everyday fabric of social intercourse, but they are not choices to adopt certain structures and ways of relating, and are thus of little interest to students of broad, qualitative social change. The distinction is between "market research," be it commercial or political, and real social theory.

Fundamental choices among alternative ways of relating do exist, however, as revealed most clearly where political alternatives, political conflict, and thus choice among choice structures, are present: in Northern Ireland, where Catholics and Protestants disagree over how to relate to one another; in the civil rights movement, which proposed to U.S. citizens an alternative way races could relate; and in the several current rebellions in Latin America. All of these are clashes over opposing ways people will relate to one another both economically and politically. In such struggles the tension arising from weighty, counter-poised reasons for alternative ways of relating makes apparent the fulcrum of choice creating this tension.

Choice is disguised in social regularity, and revealed in social change. Any theory of social change must accordingly contain at least an empirical theory of why social actors choose one way of relating and not another. Consider once again White's (1962) theory that the impersonal forces of technological change cause social change. Even if the theory were to ignore the action of human choice in the invention and development of new technologies, it must still explain why, faced with new technological possibilities (and the social changes potential in them), people will *choose* to adopt them. Thus the theory requires an embedded or attached theory of individual choice. In the case of the stirrup, the theory may be that people would always rather live dominated by mounted knights than die opposing them. Such a "theory of choice" is obviously both simple-minded and factually wrong. But the important point for the present argument is that even the most grand theories of powerful, impersonal, economic or geopolitical forces must ultimately rest on a theory of how people choose.

D.   The Choice Among Alternative Ways of Relating Is Made on Both Moral and Practical Grounds

In choosing among ways of relating, the actor finds relevant to the choice two quite distinct considerations. First is the actor's judgment of the moral[20] status of the alternative ways of relating. Ways of relating establish how people are to deal with one another; they specify what interests exist, whether these interests will be satisfied or not, and in what way. Once established as a common framework of interaction, a way of relating is prescriptive and intended to apply to all.[21] A way of relating constitutes a common moral position adopted by the people interacting through it, regardless of whether those actors see it as involving moral issues. Because a way of relating establishes how ethical questions are to be resolved, the choice among ways of relating is an ethical one.[22]

Ethics is not the only consideration relevant to the choice, however. A social actor must also consider how to establish the alternative way of relating as the norm of interaction. One can evaluate the alternatives with reference only to one's personal moral code, but the basis of *social* life is reciprocal action within the same way of relating.[23] But before action can be social, the actors must first establish which way of relating will be the norm. Each actor's choice of which way of relating to employ will thus depend not only on a moral evaluation, but also on a practical judgment of how feasible it would be to establish any of the alternatives. And feasibility depends on a world of considerations: the distribution of personal moral preferences in the group; the effort required to teach others a way of relating; and the current structural power (Stone, 1980) commanded by the proponents of various views. These varied considerations I call *practical,* because they exist apart from any single actor's normative preferences. To the extent that distinctively moral discourse is absent among the actors, these practical considerations will prevail, and strategic rather than moral consider-ations will govern the establishment of a way of relating.

The choice among ways of relating thus involves both moral and practical considerations: moral considerations of what ways of relating are right, and practical considerations of what ways of relating the actor can establish as normative. This conclusion should be familiar to the reader from the works of Weber (1958) and Mead (1962), as well as the more recent formulations of Parsons (1961). I have taken the reader over this ground again in order to clarify in what way normative evaluations are significant. I now turn to the consequences of that significance.

E.   *It Follows from D that Two Extreme Forms of Social Change Theories Can Be Distinguished, Differing in Whether They Concentrate on Practical or Normative Considerations as the Source of Social Change*

The distinction between practical and moral considerations of choice organizes social change theories along a continuum ranging from those in which social dynamics stem solely from objective social forces, at one extreme, to those in which social dynamics stem solely from the moral choices of social actors, at the other. Theories of objective social change point implicitly to the practical considerations facing people as they make and remake their ways of relating.

White's (1962) theory of social change arising from technological innovation, as cited in Section A of this chapter, is an example of one extreme. A second example can be taken from studies of the impact of communications on political change. Communications theorists (e.g., Lerner, 1958, and the authors in Pye, 1963) see the advent of new communications technologies—prototypically the transistor radio—as creating new mass demands and, in the face of institutional incapacity to satisfy those demands, mass frustration. Control over the media enables emerging national elites to make their preferred ways of relating more prominent (in particular, their desire for mass mobilization in support of the central government). As is also made clear in White's analysis of medieval technological changes, however, the new technology constrains the new elites (e.g., radio carries well only certain types of appeals) and blocks their objectives in unanticipated ways (e.g., through the mass frustration that follows rapid politicization). In these examples the new technologies act impersonally; moral choice plays no role. The national elites just mentioned, for example, had their preferred way of relating well before the advent of the transistor. Technology merely altered the mix of objective forces in the struggle of the new against the traditional elites; it did not create a new morality.

I know of no theories of social change at the other extreme of the continuum discussed here; all theories readily admit that impersonal social forces affect social change to some degree. Some theories do focus on individual moral choice to a greater degree than others, however. Gabriel Almond (1973), for example, sees development as resting on the framework of rational choices made by social actors. Almond does not specifically term these choices "moral," but the choice among different social arrangements is obviously of ethical significance, regardless of the grounds—"rational" or otherwise—on which it is made. James C. Scott (1976), who also focuses on "rational" choices of peasants, refers directly to such choices as moral. Jüergen Habermas provides the clearest example of a theory focusing on moral choice; he views social change, and particularly political development, as the consequence of direct efforts of social actors to establish and maintain a social system allowing for undistorted communication. Because communicative action raises several validity claims, Habermas calls attention to the different methods required to redeem these claims: the scientific method, to redeem the claims of (factual) "truth"; the psychoanalytic method, to redeem the claims of "truthfulness" (authenticity); and, of most concern in this essay, the methods of ethical justification, to redeem the claim of (interpersonal) "rightness."[24] Habermas argues in *Legitimation Crisis* (1975) and *Communication and the Evolution of Society* (1979:esp. Ch. 5) that people's normative evaluations of a state's legitimacy claims have a substantial, immediate impact on the stability of that state.

In principle, then, social change theories can incorporate moral choice to a greater or lesser extent. The question I now turn to is whether we can exclude moral choice altogether. In other words, can a change/i theory be complete?

F. *The Choice Among Alternative Ways of Relating Can Always Potentially Be Made on Moral Grounds*

One cannot exclude the possibility of moral choice from social change theories. To show this, I must deal with two major arguments by which moral choice is excluded: the theoretical argument that moral grounds are merely a post hoc rationalization of nonmoral processes; and the practical argument that the moral aspects of choice are swamped by the practical (nonmoral; impersonal) social forces. The theoretical argument denies the existence of moral considerations; the practical argument denies their force. Note that I need not counter these arguments by taking the opposite position—that, theoretically, all moralizing speech is genuinely moral and that, practically, moral considerations overwhelm all others. I need only argue the limited position that there does exist a domain of moral considerations and that such considerations can determine action.

The theoretical argument holds that moral speech does not indicate the existence of an autonomous moral domain, i.e., a domain of discourse with its own concerns and standards of justification. Instead, moral speech is held to exist merely to disguise from oneself or others the real basis on which one makes one's decisions: moral speech has no authenticity, because the decisions are made on quite another basis. An extreme Freudianism, for example, might hold that all moralizing is merely a papering over of subconscious urges unacceptable to the conscious mind.

This argument obviously has some validity. At some point in our lives, we have all found ourselves, through ignorance of or distaste for the real basis of our actions, justifying them by advancing arguments we didn't really believe. Ordinary observation of others tells us also that people exhibit to different degrees this tendency to rationalization. "Strong" people seem capable of reporting the real bases for their actions, so their explanations maintain the ring of truth over time; "weak" people have difficulty reporting honestly, so their explanations inevitably ring false or eventually come into question.

On the other hand, our very ability to recognize that we do occasionally (or even often) rationalize depends on our recognition of a domain of authentic speech. If we can distinguish rationalization, it must be from truthfulness. We recognize rationalization not as a natural state but as a psychological difficulty or disturbance from which we wish to free ourselves. Thus psychoanalysis is not simply diagnostic but also emancipatory; psychoanalysts do not shake their heads in sorrow at the irremediable falsity of humans but rather seek through psychoanalysis to assist people in recovering their real selves. In sum, the theoretical argument that moral speech indicates no authentic domain of discourse cannot be maintained. Moral speech cannot be taken uncritically, but our very capacity for criticism reveals the presence of a domain of authenticity.

There still remains the practical argument, however, that in the real world, nonmoral considerations of action outweigh any moral sense. This position grants that there is a domain of moral authenticity, but contends that our actual decisions are made, whatever our intentions, on other grounds. According to this position, the domain of moral authenticity may enable us to decry the actions we are forced to make and the pressures on us to make them, but it cannot alter the necessity of the actions.

It is apparent, though, that people are able to advocate and establish ways of relating they believe to be ethically right, even against practical difficulties. One need only cite great reformers like Mohandas Gandhi and Martin Luther King, Jr., to see that the practical considerations of clubs, dogs, jails, and popular antagonism are not the only social forces at work. People do occasionally make "impractical" choices on moral grounds. Although practical considerations may make moral choice painful or even fatal, the possibility and force of moral choice can never be dismissed.

G. *Any Complete Theory of Social Change Must Therefore Incorporate at Least an Empirical Theory of Moral Choice*

It follows from the above that strictly impersonal theories of change—in my terminology, change/i theories—are not tenable. Any complete theory of social change must be able to account not only for the practical forces affecting change but also for how people's moral choices affect it.

I have not yet distinguished between change/e and change/n theories, however, since the argument thus far makes no special claim about the nature of the required theory of moral choice. If we are to have an empirical/predictive theory of social change, the required, associated theory of moral choice must also be empirical/predictive in nature, but I have not yet established any necessity for it to capture the normativeness of the choice.[25]

H. *It Follows from C, D, and F that Any Complete Theory of Social Change Must Incorporate a Theory of How Social Actors Evaluate the Virtue of Alternative Ways of Relating*

If an adequate theory of social change requires at least an empirical theory of moral choice, what sort of demands do we make on the latter theory? Such a theory must account for two different types of moral choices: choice within a way of relating and choice between ways of relating. Choice *within* a way of relating has to do with the ordinary course of meaningful social action; choice *between* ways of relating has to do with the very structures through which social action acquires meaning.

To describe choice within a way of relating is simply to describe moral reasoning itself. When established as the basis of a relationship, a way of relating is normatively prescriptive. Deciding what the prescription means—and how, therefore, one should satisfy it—is moral reasoning. Thus a theory of moral choice must at a minimum describe the nature and forms of moral reasoning itself, or equivalently, the possible ways of relating.

Not all moral choices arise within a mutually accepted way of relating, however. Occasionally social actors must choose between alternative ways of relating. Such choice may occur when an actor is able to visualize several alternative ways of relating with others in a situation (possibly including completely novel ways of relating), or when different actors simply meet and wish to employ different ways of relating. As noted previously, the choice among ways of relating is itself in part a moral choice, and so a complete theory of moral choice must describe how such choices are made.

I. *It Follows from F that Empirical Theories of Actors' Moral Evaluations Must Capture the Normativeness of the Choice*

The theory of culture to a large extent disentangles the description of human life from moral judgments. Yet, since moral judgment is integral to human experience, an amoral approach cannot do full justice to this experience and indeed disrupts its phenomenological integrity (Metzger, 1981:ix–xxv).

I claim in this section that a purely empirical theory of moral choice—that is, one that describes moral choice as a consequence of nonmoral factors—is impossible. The argument proceeds by contradiction. Suppose that one *were* able to predict on exclusively empirical and nonmoral grounds people's moral choices—for example, on the basis of their greediness, their reptilian hindbrain, or their mothers' having dropped them on their heads at birth. That theory must also apply reflexively, that is, to oneself. One is then in a situation in which one claims that one's own moral choices are made on nonmoral grounds. This position is untenable, however, because it is vulnerable to the so-called "open question": "But is it *right* that I make reptilian moral decisions?" This is a meaningful question because we have assumed that the theory is based on nonmoral considerations.[26] The open question may be posed either by others or by oneself, but in either case it demands a response. One's possible responses are to (a) do nothing, since morality has no autonomy from empirical forces; (b) change one's definition of morality so that it is coterminous with the empirical theory; or (c) alter one's behavior.[27] But none of these responses is satisfactory. I disposed of (a) earlier: morality is not an epiphenomenon or post hoc rationalization of nonmoral considerations. Response (b) violates our initial assumption that the empirical theory is based on nonmoral considerations. Response (c) contradicts our assumption that the empirical theory predicts moral choice, since one has chosen to behave not according to the theory. Thus our original assumption, that an empirical theory of moral choice can be constructed on exclusively nonmoral grounds, is untenable.

J.   It Follows from I that Only Change/n Theories Are Tenable

The basic point is that if morality is a quasi-autonomous domain, then a theory of moral choice must take into account to some degree the authentically moral considerations involved in moral choice. A theory of moral choice applies to us as well as our subjects. If we are to treat our subjects as respectfully as ourselves, our theory of moral choice must capture the normativeness of their choices, not just the choices alone.[28] Change/e theories are therefore not tenable, and any complete theory of social change must incorporate a normatively grounded theory of moral choice.

Of the many possible empirical theories of moral choice, that of Kohlberg (1981, 1984) appears to have the most solid normative grounding. Kohlberg's theory of the development of moral reasoning can be applied (with some care to avoid the composition fallacy) to groups of people sharing a common way of relating. The result (*DPD*; Rosenberg, Ward, and Chilton, 1988: Chapter 6; see also Power and Reimer, 1978) is a normatively grounded conception of political development rooted in Kohlberg's empirically well-established theory. A similar approach is taken by Radding (1985), who explains certain historical changes in terms of Piaget's analysis of the development of abstract logical reasoning. Piaget's claims are of logical adequacy, while Kohlberg's are of moral adequacy, but the theoretical issues raised are quite similar.[29]

K.   It Follows from J that Conceptions of Development Must Be Normatively Grounded

If social scientists are then to take moral discourse seriously, we must accept as valid our discourse about which social system is best for a society, or, at least, which is better than the present one. (There is no implication here that what is better or best will be the same for every society.) Since any complete theory of social change must incorporate a normatively grounded theory of moral choice, we have to recognize the meaningfulness of the assertion that a society has become better. Our natural language term for a society's change from one configuration to a normatively superior one is development: we say that the society has developed.[30]

L.   Implications for Social Science

Almost two decades ago, Huntington (1971) proposed that social scientists abandon the normatively loaded study of development and take up instead the purely empirical study of "change." The thrust of my argument, however, is that normative considerations are inevitably a factor in social change, so that the vision of a strictly empirical theory of social change is an illusion. Every complete theory of social change must also include a theory of the nature and circumstances of development. Certainly some social changes are morally neutral, or arise from nonmoral causes. But to the extent that moral choice does have force in the world, some social change will be developmental in nature.

The examples cited above are of large-scale social movements, but normative choice may have as great or greater an effect on small-scale interactions. James C. Scott (1985) describes the tension between the large-scale structural power of the landlord and the small-scale moral expectations and traditions of the peasants, in which tension the peasants have recourse to the "weapons of the weak." Similarly, Tilly (1978:186, citing E. P. Thompson, 1971) sees the nineteenth-century European social conflicts over the price of staple foods as moral conflicts concerning the proper relationship among producers, consumers, and governmental authorities. Such small-scale conflicts, if pervasive enough, can generate large-scale movements, but it is clear that moral choice is important at all scales of social activity. Social scientists thus cannot rely upon a "division of labor" argument to avoid studying moral choice: all levels of social activity appear drenched in such choice.

Some social scientists might still take the position that moral choice is not important enough in comparison to nonmoral considerations to warrant attention. If social science can explain (say) 99 percent of all explainable variance by nonmoral factors, why should it enter the mine field of morality to explain the remaining 1 percent?

An obvious answer is that the relative importance of moral and nonmoral factors cannot be estimated unless both are examined. We will never know what percentage of the variance moral factors explain unless we look at them.

But assume that the figure of 1 percent is correct. A restriction of social change theories to nonmoral factors would still affect the character of social science—in particular, by making it conservative instead of emancipatory. Let me quickly define those terms: a conservative social science is one that gives no scope to moral intentions. It is conservative not in the sense of preserving the past, because it sees many potential nonmoral sources of change, but rather in the sense of denying the possibility of a willed emancipation. It is conservative in its denial of the possibility of progress, since humans are the helpless victims of forces beyond themselves. An emancipatory social science, on the other hand, specifically recognizes the possibility of moral choice. A normatively grounded theory of moral choice allows social scientists legitimately to adopt a specifically critical posture vis-à-vis alternative social futures. It recognizes and raises to consciousness both the impersonal forces a society experiences and the moral considerations that the choice among futures raises.

In essence, then, social scientists must choose one of two visions of their project: on the one hand, a social science that disempowers people by denying the possibility they can change anything (or, to cast this as this project's adherents might, that liberates people from the dashed hopes attendant on a misguided faith in moral agency); and on the other hand, a social science that recognizes the possibility of moral change and ultimately of human emancipation (at the cost of the frustrations and conflicts of normative discourse).

Two considerations argue that only the latter choice makes sense. First and most direct, people already make, and know deep down they can always already make, moral choices—that they are not victims. A *complete* social science must recognize that.

Even in the face of the first argument one could continue to maintain that the role of moral choice is so slight, and its threat to our self-conception as scientists so immediate, that we are justified and even obligated to neglect it. We are comfortable with our long-established role as "scientists" and all too aware of the hubris tinging the role of prophet, visionary, or moralist. And yet this argument seems to depend at heart on our willed ignorance of the role of moral choice, not on a realistic assessment of the dangers of the different paths. We can choose to remain "scientists" in the narrow sense only if we are sure that moral choice is really of little consequence; but this is not at all certain. Each side sees what it wants to see: "scientists," ignoring the role of moral choice, devise experiments showing less and less role for it; "emancipators" discover, by contrast, that the more scope they provide for recognizing and making possible moral choice, the more important it seems to become. My second argument is cast in the face of this uncertainty: that when one cannot choose between two alternatives on the basis of clear evidence or logic, then one should choose the alternative with the more interesting consequences. If one ultimately decides that the consequences are not really very interesting, or if the evidence really does mount up in the opposite direction, one has lost no more than time and has by recompense acquired a firmer understanding of why the other alternative is superior. But to foreclose options without looking at them seems to me to be a grave crime, a crime only made worse by the excuse that we are afraid of ourselves. This second argument is less direct but I believe more persuasive than the first.

Given our uncertainty of evidence and logic, the only reasonable alternative is to admit and examine the possibility that moral choice is important and that human emancipation is possible, and to look vigorously for how it might appear and be fostered. Obviously we will have to remain conscious of the many pitfalls of such a stance—notably, the possibility that real emancipation will be swamped by charlatanry, moral imperialism, and muddy thinking. Our self-definition as scientists has not protected us from these pitfalls. My own sense is that a determined respect for bottom-up emancipation, however, as found in liberation theology or in Paulo Friere's "pedagogy of the oppressed," will provide sufficient moral compass.

In conclusion, it seems to me that people already know that they can make moral choices—that they are not victims. If social scientists do not take up the challenge of explaining to them where and what their choices are, then other, less thoughtful—or less scrupulous—people will. As long as the emancipation of all people lies ahead of us, social scientists have as clear a charter as anyone, and better than most, to create it. We should welcome the challenge instead of running from it.

Notes

1. I agree with Huntington's argument here to the extent that if, as he claims, we cannot reach agreement on the nature of development, we should stop talking about it. My claim is, of course, that the conception in *DPD* is the basis of agreement.

2. Such a usage is seen in Wellhofer's (1989) article, "The Comparative Method and the Study of Development, Diffusion, and Social Change." Even though the term development is singular in the title, its meaning in the article does not go beyond that of an inevitable process (in particular, of industrialization).

3. Normative evaluations of teleological developments are like evaluations of the law of gravity. We might prefer that gravity be stronger, or weaker, or more variable, but such evaluations are irrelevant to gravity itself. Normative evaluations of alternative forms of society, on the other hand, are quite relevant to the political-developmental process.

4. This is the argument of dependency theorists, who argue that development consequent on the rise of capitalism in Western Europe does not carry over to the penetration of capitalism into underdeveloped countries today.

5. Palmer (1989:Table 2.1) lists an enormous variety of changes that appear to be associated with development.

6. Indeed, in my opinion, normative grounding has been the reef on which our predecessors' theoretical ships have sunk, either because other theorists would not accept the normative premises (implicit or explicit), or because the societies they purported to describe would not choose as they were supposed to. Huntington (1965) suffered at least the first fate; most development planners have suffered the second.

7. Edwards (1989:1) similarly argues that because "the theory is a factor" and "the theorist is an actor," we must move away from theory as prediction and toward theory

as creation. Edwards asserts (1989:14) that this reflexivity ultimately falsifies *all* theories, but this is an overstatement: reflexivity falsifies only those theories that are not normatively grounded.

8. Unless otherwise specified, "we" in this article means all social scientists (political scientists, economists, sociologists, anthropologists, social psychologists, cultural geographers, philologists) working in the area of social change and development.

9. Any theory of social change is obviously also a theory of social stasis, since a complete explanation of change will also explain the occurrence of stasis as the absence of change.

10. For the example's sake I am casting White's view of social change in a more extreme way than he probably intends.

11. For example, an act of moral courage could be explained as the consequence of being raised in a certain social class.

12. Hudelson (1990) discusses the historical variety of theories termed "scientific Marxism."

13. I use the term "advancement" advisedly: Hobhouse has no doubt that, in the long run, our moral systems have gotten better and better.

14. This trichotomy of approaches to social change resembles in part the distinction made by Charles Tilly (1978:6, citing James Coleman, 1973:1–5) between "causal" and "purposive" explanations of social action. While change/i theories are clearly causal, Tilly does not distinguish purposive explanations resting on nonmoral, empirical theories of choice (change/e) from purposive explanations resting on the nature of morality itself (change/n).

15. This distinction is, of course, that of Clifford Geertz (1973) between "thick" and "thin" descriptions.

16. The choice may not be of whether to relate, as with Al and Bob above, but it will always be among alternative ways to relate. In a larger sense, the choice of whether or not to relate is itself a choice of a relationship. This is the crux of the issue of how we are to relate to the starving peoples of the world: ignoring their problems is only a more horrible alternative.

17. I must widen the connotation of my terms here. To agree on a way of relating sounds like an agreement among the parties immediately present in some transaction: e.g., if a candidate buys a citizen's vote, the way of relating established appears to concern only them. But it is evident that their action violates the basic relationship among all voters, whose physical presence is not required (and was not even contemplated) by the general way of relating we call voting. Bribing voters destroys the meaning of all social life predicated on the sharing of that understanding. Thus Gandhian nonviolent resisters accept legal punishment for their actions in order to uphold the ideal of a shared understanding even while they try to change its form (Bondurant, 1971, esp. Ch. 5).

18. Palmer (1989:111–113), for example, carefully distinguishes coups d'etat and revolutions on precisely this basis. He also notes in this vein (p. 252) Ghana's (quickly suppressed) post-coup song entitled, "The Cars Are the Same, Only the Drivers Have Changed."

19. Historically, we have seen yesterday's blood feud become today's political and economic competition. Intimate, personal ties of community have become contractual and impersonal. These changes have not been cosmetic or superficial: rather, they have altered radically the way people in Western society look at and relate to one another.

20. The term moral can mean either "evaluable against standards of morality" or "in accord with standards of morality." The former sense notes the mere presence of a claim; the latter sense requires a redemption of that claim. In this article, the former sense is meant unless the latter sense is specified.

21. Of course, "all" is limited to the people who the way of relating contemplates as interacting. The Rotary Club's way of relating, for example, binds only Rotarians.

22. I hasten to add that I am not positing here the empirical existence of any single system of moral choice. Each culture (and, ultimately, each person) has a unique understanding of what is "right." But note, as Kohlberg (1981) points out, that the empirical observation that people differ in their moral judgments does not imply the philosophical conclusion that their judgments or modes of judgment are of equal merit. To maintain such an implication is a form of the naturalistic fallacy.

23. If I register to vote, for example, I do so in expectation of others doing the same; voting is a social action because everyone's action contemplates others following the same rules.

24. The terms in quotes are those employed by Thomas McCarthy, the translator of Habermas (1979).

25. By "capture the normativeness of the choice" I mean to suggest a theory that explains moral choice by reference to the nature of morality itself, not to nonmoral considerations. (Recall the discussion in Section A of change/n theories.)

26. It is one thing to claim that one's reptilian moral decisions *are* moral; it is quite another to claim that one makes reptilian moral decisions even though they *aren't* moral.

27. I ignore a fourth alternative: that while nonmoral forces inevitably and irremediably push and pull other people, they do not affect oneself. Aside from its condescension, such a position ultimately abandons the field of moral discourse itself.

28. The old joke goes: "They have prejudices; you have opinions; I have a philosophy."

29. Radding (1985) concentrates on specific historical analysis and does not fully confront the composition fallacy and the philosophical establishment of logical adequacy; *DPD* does the reverse.

30. The term "progress" could also be used, but to my mind its connotation of unilinear change is too great a burden on its use. Of course the same charge can be made against the term, "development," but we have to employ *some* term for morally grounded change, and the connotations of "development" are to my mind a lighter burden than those of "progress" or related terms.

4

Other Suggested Fundamental Theoretical Requirements

As I noted in Chapter 2, Section II.D, people are free to suggest their own FTRs. Two of my colleagues have done so, one (James Caporaso) by writing me to propose another FTR, the other (Han S. Park) by discussing explicitly the general form of political development in his *Human Needs and Political Development* (1984). I present these proposed FTRs below, arguing for most of these proposals that they should not be added to the five existing FTRs.

A. Laws of Development?

Caporaso suggests that "ability to discover laws of development" should also be an FTR. This can be taken in two senses. In the first sense, this asks that our definition of development be operationalizable (at least ideally), so that *if* there are laws of development, we can (again, ideally) discover them. In the second sense, this *requires* that an acceptable definition of development yield law-like regularities.

The first sense is indeed an FTR. It expresses the principle that concepts that cannot be operationalized, at least ideally, cannot be the basis of a scientific theory. But while I have no objection to the inclusion of such an FTR, it seems to be implicit, and perhaps even explicit, in the first three FTRs: locus of development, recognition of development, and exact specification.[1]

The second sense, insisting that there *be* laws of development, is both too strong and too weak to be an FTR: too strong, in that it makes a strong empirical assumption about development's law-like nature; too weak, because it is evaluated not on the basis of any clear evidence as to whether in fact such laws exist but instead on whether theorists have given up the search for laws. In other words, this second sense violates both of the previous chapter's "metacriteria": FTRs should make no assumptions about empirical reality, and they should be dichotomous in nature. The statement that definitions of development should enable us to discover laws of development is certainly a common wish or expectation; it cannot be a requirement by which we are willing to have our conceptualizations stand or fall.

B. The Definition Must Be Ideal, Not Empirical?

To my knowledge, Park's (1984) is the only work except *DPD* to bring abstract/

theoretical considerations directly to bear on the definition of political development. Park's discussion implicitly (and, in Chapter II, explicitly) proposes several potential FTRs.[2]

One I accept: Park argues that development must be defined as "an ideal type in the Weberian sense . . . rather than an empirically derived description of the observed society" (1984:51; see also 44). Our sense of development is far richer than any one society, so we need analysis instead of empirical description to discover its meaning. To state this in another way, no society so clearly exemplifies development that we need think only about the society and not about the concept—or at any rate, we can feel no certainty about any candidate society.

The conception of development in *DPD* meets the FTR, because development is defined there in cognitive-structural terms, not in terms of "reasoning found in Society X." An inquiry into the degree to which any society employs certain moral reasoning to structure its social relations—and thus into the degree to which that society is developed—becomes, then, an empirical exercise only.

C. The Definition Must Allow
Development Beyond Current Societies?

Citing Holsti (1975:829), Park (1984:11–12, 43–44, 52) asserts that we must "distinguish between what is modern and what is Western" (p.11) and that "the persistence of change in so-called 'developed' societies argues against this idea [that these societies represent the zenith of development]" (p.12).[3]

These assertions are certainly plausible. I think most people would agree that Western societies can benefit from further development and that they therefore do not define modernity (if we take modernity to mean the highest state of development). But the widespread agreement with this empirical judgment does not validate Park's assertions as FTRs. We have already agreed in the previous section that development must be defined without reference to any specific society. We have no business going beyond that "hands-off" FTR to the "hands-on" empirical claim that Western societies *cannot* represent the zenith of development.

D. Conceptual Universality?

Park (1984:42) argues that since societies and social change are universal and development is one type of social change, a definition of development must be universally applicable. Though the logic here is not airtight—it is conceivable that development is not universal even though change is—the conclusion certainly seems correct.[4] Thus the new FTR would read that a definition of development must apply to all forms of society.

I certainly accept this FTR,[5] and the definition advanced in *DPD* satifies it. As I will argue in Chapter 6, every society has ways of relating, and the system used to evaluate developmental stages is equally applicable to all people.

E.   Development Must Be a Teleological Process?

According to Park, development is a teleological (goal-directed) process. "Development occurs as movement over time toward the desired state of the living structure. . . . A movement in the process of development represents an incremental progression toward the achievement of a goal" (Park, 1984:48–49). Later, he argues that "in order for the explanation of development to be feasible, the developmental unit should be an entity that has inherent motivations toward the achievement of goals" (Park, 1984:51).

I disagree that development *must* proceed toward a goal. Some systems are indeed homeostatic, and many human practices and institutions are specifically goal-oriented. But this is not the only possible form of development. For example, the biological evolution of species is process-, not goal-oriented. Species have no image of what they want to become as they adapt to new conditions; they simply experiment and discover what works. Sometimes it is possible to look back at a developmental progression and view it as "seeking" its end point, but this reconstruction can only be retrospective, never predictive. Since there are senses of development both teleological and not, Park needs to eliminate all competitors to justify his FTR of development as a teleological process.

F.   Humans Must Be the Locus of Development?

Park (1984) advances two reasons that human beings should be the unit of analysis in any definition of development. First, he argues that in "order for the explanation of development to be feasible, the developmental unit should be an entity that has inherent motivations toward the achievement of goals. Thus, a human, rather than an institution, might be preferred as a unit of analysis" (Park, 1984:51–52). If we change "might be preferred as a unit of analysis," which removes any bite from the argument, to "must be the unit of analysis," we have a straightforward FTR.

Park goes on to argue that the origins of the term development also require humans to be the locus of development:

> The term "development" originated as a description of structural changes in living organisms, and it has commonly been applied to living systems. This suggests . . . that human beings need to be the unit of analysis in a developmental theory and that, therefore, the definition of political development should be in human terms (Park, 1984:52).

Again, if we elide "This suggests . . . that," we have another straightforward argument for this proposed FTR.

However, the two arguments are both weak. The first argument arises from Park's sense of development as a teleological process, which I disputed in Section E of this chapter on the grounds that development can be process-oriented as well as goal-oriented. Piagetian development is the former, and before Park could establish his FTR, he would have to advance reasons why that form of development is not feasible. The second argument fails for a similar reason: Park's argument implicitly assumes that humans are the only entity that can develop politically as living systems do. My argument is that cultures can also do so. Granted, cultures are created by humans, but this creation is collective, not individual.[6]

G. Conclusion

All FTRs suggested to me are either already satisfied by the definition of development advanced in *DPD,* or fail themselves to be adequately justified. The metacriterion that FTRs must make no empirical assumptions was especially useful in evaluating the proposals.[7]

Of course this success in handling these suggested FTRs does not in itself prove the validity of *DPD's* conception of development. As always, other theorists are free to propose and justify FTRs that may invalidate *DPD's* approach. Until such FTRs emerge, however, this approach remains unchallenged.

Notes

1. Park (1984:51) argues in this first sense that a definition "needs to be made in such a way as to facilitate the formulation of explanatory-predictive laws."
2. "The following set of criteria are formed by examining the concept from the perspective of the philosophy of science and in terms of the semantics of 'development' itself" (Park, 1984:43).
3. Park (1984:52) later summarizes his point as follows:

> In order to be nomothetic, a stage theory should account for the further development of what have been inappropriately termed "developed" societies. Here, some type of cyclical theory might be suggested as a more powerful one than a linear progressive theory under the assumption that development of human society is not to be terminated.

As discussed in the text, the first sentence is plausible but probably not an FTR. The second sentence, however, strikes me as completely implausible. Park seems to feel that only two trajectories of development are possible: the terminated linear trajectory and the cyclical. There is at least one other possibility: that development is an endless linear trajectory. To establish his claim, then, Park would have to exclude this possibility as well. My guess is that Park's intent was to challenge the complacent acceptance of Western society as the terminus of development, an intention I share.
4. I argue in the previous chapter that developmental change is possible in every society. This conclusion, if correct, closes the potential hole in Park's argument and explains why I accept his conclusion.
5. In Chapter 6, two of the FTRs applied to the concept of political culture are termed "unrestricted applicability" (FTR 6) and "nonreductionism" (FTR 7).
6. I am not entirely clear how Park's "methodological individualism" (Park, 1984:47) would view "publicly common ways of relating"—my definition of culture. Such a definition appears to me to go beyond the individual, but perhaps Park would

accept it on the grounds that culture would have, as he puts it, "no emergent qualities ... that the individual cannot alter" (Park, 1984:47), with "individual" here understood to include individuals collectively. If Park's methodological individualism includes culture, then we have no argument. However, I believe Park's phrasing tends to mislead the reader into thinking solely of the isolated individual, and so I must assume that Park does *not* view culture as meeting the conditions of methodological individualism.

    7. I have observed an unaware mixing of the empirical and the theoretical in many areas of social science conceptualizing.

5

Two Recent Conceptions of Political Development

We are now in a position to apply these five FTRs to the two conceptions of political development offered by Han Park (1984) and Harry Eckstein (1982). Since these theorists attempted to conceptualize political development without starting from any explicit set of FTRs, much less the five given here, it would be unreasonable to expect their formulations to address directly these FTRs. Consequently, the analysis will focus on the degree to which the two conceptions imply in some natural way a means of satisfying the FTRs.

I. Han S. Park (1984): *Human Needs and Political Development: A Dissent to Utopian Solutions*

Han Park's formal definition of political development is as follows: "Political development may be defined in terms of the capacity of the political system to satisfy the changing needs of the members of the society" (Park, 1984:58). The needs Park postulates are, in order from developmentally lowest to highest, the quasi-Maslovian needs of "survival," "belongingness," "leisure," and "control." Institutions are therefore said to be faced with the respective tasks of "regime formation," "political integration," "resource expansion," and "conflict management" (Park, 1984: Chapter 3).

This formal definition conflicts with Park's informal definition of development as the change from institutions which satisfy a lower need to those which satisfy a higher need.[1] According to the formal definition, the following would be a developmental advance: a shift from institutions that were moderately able to satisfy people's control needs, on the one hand, to institutions that were powerfully able to satisfy people's survival needs, on the other. Because the capacity increased, so did development, even though the individual need that was satisfied retrogressed (by the informal definition) from one end of the hierarchical scale to the other.

Any subsequent discussion will obviously be conditioned on which of these two definitions of development one assumes to be Park's "real" definition. Since I wish to give the most plausible reading to the works, I will assume that Park intends what I call his informal definition, not his formal definition; I think the informal is the better definition.[2]

49

The informal definition satisfies the FTR of exact specification: political development is defined directly, rather than as the consequence of some cause, the cause of some consequence, the correlate of some substitute indicator, or some broader process of which only a part is named.

Park wavers between locating development in terms of the characteristics of individuals (and aggregates of those characteristics), on the one hand, and characteristics of institutions, on the other. He wants to adhere to a doctrine of "methodological individualism" (Park, 1984:46–48, 59), but in Park's definition the locus of development is institutions. This wavering produces some confusion for the reader but no real problem with the locus of development, as far as I can tell; Park simply seems to have confused his empirical theory of the origins of development, which he plausibly locates in the (aggregated) needs of individuals, with his theoretical definition of development, which he locates in institutions.

But this wavering does have negative consequences when one examines Park's work in light of the FTR of the micro–macro connection. Park tries to make the micro–macro connection by defining political development as institutional change resulting from individual change. But he thereby mixes an empirical with an analytical/definitional claim. If development is the movement toward a certain class of institutions (i.e., those with the capacity for satisfying high-level needs), then it is unclear how the mere emergence of those institutions will produce associated differences in the people who operate them. Even if social institutions are oriented to the satisfaction of certain high-level needs, why must their subjects suddenly feel those needs? If one attempts to handle this problem by locating development in the upward shift of the aggregate needs themselves (i.e., defining the individual instead of the institution as the locus of development), it is still unclear how the mere shift in those needs will in and of itself produce changes in institutions. (It may, for example, merely create greater regime repression.) Park very handily assumes that higher needs will be associated with more-developed institutions, but the connection is empirical (and assumed), not analytical/definitional.

A strength of Park's definition is its clear answer to the FTR of the recognition of development. Park lays out in successive chapters the different institutions that can satisfy the four needs. Using a variety of examples from widely different cultural traditions, he attempts to maintain a focus on the abstract problem of satisfying those needs rather than on any particular set of institutional arrangements.[3]

Despite Park's admirable determination to prevent ethnocentrism, his conception nevertheless fails to satisfy the FTR of normative grounding. Park's position vis-à-vis his normative claims is unclear. On the one hand, he uses moral terms to discuss institutions in the context of their satisfying higher-level needs. Early in his postscript, for example, he says that his vision of eventual developmental retrogression is one of "the moral decay of human society"(p. 260). But he is not comfortable with this moral language. On the next page (p. 261) he declares, "The incremental progression of human wants was not meant to be a normative imperative. . . . If there were to be a normative concept of development, it would be anything but the definition offered in this book." Park distinguishes what he calls base needs, like security and belongingness, from moral needs rooted in mutuality and communication. Park feels he has written, in other words, an empirical analysis of what social change has looked like (and may continue to look like), not a normative vision of what development should be.

I believe Park shortchanges himself, however. The different needs he cites may not represent the heights of human experience, but there still seems to be grounds to choose among them. To take the most obvious example, the human interactions arising from a preoccupation exclusively with basic survival would seem to be much less desirable than those arising from a concern for belongingness.[4] Park's formulations are at least susceptible to moral scrutiny, even if he chooses not to pursue this issue.

Unfortunately, Park's last two stages are both less believable and less susceptible to normative grounding than the first two stages. It is difficult to see what normative grounds would make the social relations stemming from a need for leisure (and, at the next stage, for control) superior to those stemming from the need for belongingness. Park himself recognizes this difficulty in his postscript, where he laments the loss of social solidarity and the rise of zero-sum institutions. He then returns to his position that the need hierarchy is an empirical fact and not a scale of moral desirability, but supplies no justification for that claim. Although Park starts by viewing the need hierarchy as an assumption, he ends by regarding it as an established fact. On page 61, the hierarchy is given merely as a "suggestion"; on page 81, people are "believed" to have an inherent need for leisure after the needs for survival and belongingness are satisfied; and on page 187, "the structure of human needs is such that . . . the need for leisure will emerge." But it is not plausible that the many complex institutions Park studies arise merely from a common need for leisure. The institutions may produce leisure as a by-product, but I cannot see leisure itself as their organizing spirit.[5]

II.   Harry Eckstein (1982): "The Idea of Political Development: From Dignity to Efficiency"

Harry Eckstein defines political development as the growth that occurs "in politics as such" (p. 470), and elaborates what this growth looks like and how it arises. His definition satisfies the FTR of exact specification: he defines development directly, not as the cause inferred from a more clearly identified consequence, as the consequence deduced from a more clearly identified cause, as the unseen correlate of a more clearly identified phenomenon, or as a broad process of which the identified phenomenon is but one constituent aspect.

Eckstein waffles slightly between defining the growth of politics as the growth of the "princely domain," on the one hand, and defining it as the growth of all "relations that involve, say, legitimate power, or conflict management, or the regulation of social conduct, and the like," on the other.[6] But this does not strike me as a serious conceptual problem, partly because in his later analysis Eckstein sticks closely to the former conception, and partly because the distinction doesn't seem particularly important.[7]

Eckstein's definition does not specify the locus of development, because it is not clear what "politics as such" consists of.[8] He gives a number of elaborations of the term (p. 470): "the political domain of society"; "political authority and competition for politically allocated values"; in "Durkheim's terminology, . . . 'political density,' perhaps as a special aspect of a growing 'moral density'"; "political interactions [as opposed to] nonpolitical interactions"; and "the functions and activities of [the clearly defined domain] of the heads of societies, the princes, chiefs, or kings." These sound clear enough, but as one gets closer to them, their outlines blur. Is "politics as such" a characteristic of individuals—for example, the proportion or variety of their interactions affected by government? Or, on the other hand, is "politics as such" a characteristic of political institutions—for example, their size and complexity, the nature of their claims, or the mix of resources they command?

Eckstein, like Park, attempts to finesse the FTR of the micro–macro connection. His treatment of the domain of politics tries to appropriate both micro and macro aspects of society simultaneously. He is concerned about the claims made by political institutions, but he is also concerned that these claims be accepted by individuals. To put this another way, it is not clear whether politics is primarily the domain of the rulers and the political institutions through which they rule, or the domain of those who acquiesce in or support the rulers' claims.[9] Eckstein seems to regard the domain of the rulers as more important, since he includes several passages that assert that the rulers can simply overpower the others.[10] His ambiguity on this point also clouds Eckstein's functionalist discussion of why development occurs. This functionalism appears when he says, "The general motive force at work in the sequence of stages . . . is surely the drive for the direct and indirect benefit of 'efficient' primacy in and over society" (p. 484), and again when he says, "it is clear that struggles for establishing an 'efficient' principal domain are only resolved when an urgent societal need for such resolution arises" (p. 485). This sounds impressive, but just whose "drive" is at work? Who, exactly, is feeling the "need for such resolution?" By failing to specify the critical actors (that is, failing to clarify the locus of development), Eckstein disguises the micro–macro problem: his formulations imply that social changes arise automatically out of the society's collective recognition of its own need for, and consequent drive for, the establishment of an efficient princely domain.

Eckstein's conception does satisfy the FTR of the recognition of development, specifying both abstractly and with historical examples the developmental stages.[11]

In order to satisfy the FTR of normative grounding, Eckstein would have to argue that each successive means of satisfying the functional needs for greater efficiency was normatively better than the previous means. Such an argument would most likely have to rely on some sort of utilitarian theory of morality in order to convert a collective good into a moral imperative binding on society's members.[12] Making this argument would require Eckstein to specify what collective benefits arise from each stage and why each stage's basket of collective goods is to be preferred to the previous stage's basket. Assuming that such an argument could be made, there would appear to be two difficulties with it. The first difficulty is the validity of the utilitarian position itself, which seems to me to have been effectively criticized by Rawls. The second difficulty is that Eckstein himself seems ambivalent about the benefits attached to efficiency: in his conclusion, he mentions a desire for a return from the politics of efficiency to that of dignity. If efficiency is morally preferable to dignity, from whence arises this desire for a return to dignity, and on what basis will he be able to dismiss it as having a lesser moral weight?

III.   Conclusion

Both Park and Eckstein attempt to define political development in culture-free terms, and in particular as the result of universal needs and forces. The universality of these needs and forces certainly avoids the theoretical pitfalls of simple theories of "Westernization" or "modernity," and the variety of these needs and forces yields a culturally diverse set of institutional forms and developmental dynamics. Both conceptions take care to specify the sequence of social stages, including the possibility of development of Western society beyond its current state. Certainly the two analysts attempt to define political development in a theoretically conscious way. Both conceptions satisfy the FTR of exact specification, which means both have the courage to make a direct statement about development. Beyond this, the theorists start not simply by asserting their definitions but instead by discussing the theoretical problems associated with development. Park in particular has attempted to examine political development as a concept independent of the research tradition bearing its name. This gives him an independence of thought that is most refreshing to a field whose intellectual heritage is increasingly problematic.[13] This independence of thought is also reflected in Park's attempt to look at development as a methodologist; the first two chapters of his book present a theoretical analysis of the development concept, culminating in a list of Park's own FTRs.[14] Development studies need more such theoretically guided analyses.

Unfortunately, both conceptions fail to satisfy the two hardest FTRs: normative grounding and the micro–macro connection. This failure is shared with most other political development theory, because both FTRs raise very touchy political issues. The touchiness of normative grounding is obvious, and the micro–macro connection raises touchy questions about the mechanisms of social power whereby people come to acquiesce in social institutions they neither like nor create. Perhaps as a result of this touchiness, mainstream political science rarely confronts these issues directly. Social scientists' common professional stance of value neutrality makes them particularly loathe to deal with normative grounding. And although the micro–macro connection has been the direct concern of symbolic interactionists, their work remains outside the mainstream of political science.

The overall conclusion we can draw from the above analysis is that the FTRs are useful in analyzing previous conceptions and helping theorists notice where and why these conceptions have difficulties. The FTRs are practical aids to theoretical discourse.

Notes

1. Park (1984:Chapter 3). This change presumably occurs in response to a change in the aggregate need level in the society.
2. Choosing the formal definition would simply lead to worse theoretical difficulties around the issue of normative grounding.
3. Park's Figure 10 (p. 168), for example, includes theorists as diverse as Thomas Jefferson, Kim Il-Sung, Indira Gandhi, and Syngman Rhee in an attempt to understand possible ideological means of achieving political integration to satisfy the need for belongingness.
4. Aronoff (1967) describes how on St. Kitts, different need levels result in different social interactions. No one reading Aronoff's analysis would remain insensitive to the difference between the social world of a typical St. Kitts cane cutter and that of a fisherman.
5. I believe that Park's difficulty with the last two needs in his hierarchy arises because they do not match the corresponding stages (or any other stages, for that matter) in Maslow's need hierarchy. Park might think of looking for inspiration to Maslow's need hierarchy, or to McClelland's work on the need for Achievement, or to Weber's work on the Protestant Ethic. I believe these would be fairly readily susceptible to normative interpretation.
6. Eckstein goes on to say, "In that case, 'politics' may simply exist throughout society and not be located in any clearly defined social domain or institution" (p. 470).
7. Eckstein makes the distinction "to avoid confusion about what is being argued here," but ends his discussion by noting that the two phenomena "occur in conjunction" (p. 470).
8. Nancy Fraser (1989) notes that the demarcation of politics from other spheres is theoretically suspect:

> I shall treat the terms "political," "economic" and "domestic" as cultural classifications and ideological labels rather than as designations of structures, spheres or things. . . . Let me begin by noting that the terms "politics" and "political" are highly contested and they have a number of different senses. . . . In general, there are no a priori constraints dictating that some matters simply are intrinsically political and others simply are intrinsically not. . . . However, it would be misleading to suggest that, for any society in any period, the boundary between what is political and what is not is simply fixed or given (Fraser, 1989:7–8).

9. I should also note that Eckstein does not address the conceptual problem of identifying who the real rulers of a society are. He takes for granted that the appearance of power is the reality. If, for example, the various Marxian, elitist, and neo-elitist arguments are correct, we should be looking not at governmental but at economic elites. Thus Eckstein's concept of "the political" smuggles empirical assumptions about the nature of power into what seems at first glance a merely theoretical definition of the concept.

10. "In [power] struggles the princely domain has overwhelming resources for subduing rivals and enlarging its effective control over society. [Such resources include the leaders'] representation of societies [to themselves,] links to the supernatural, . . a universal social need for adjudication, and, again, a 'natural' tendency to associate that necessary function with society's embodiments" (pp. 474–475).

"Substantive primacy . . . is . . . a supremely valuable resource for acquiring additional resources" (p. 479).

"The primacy of a social domain above other domains and, even more, the 'distancing' of courts from societies, inevitably lead to a conception of princely power and social order . . . as being somehow unrelated" (p. 481).

"The general motive force at work in the sequence of stages . . . is surely the drive for the direct and indirect benefits of 'efficient' primacy in and over society—the direct benefit of social elevation and indirect perquisites, such as material goods" (p. 484).

"Thus, while struggles for primacy propel politics throughout developmental time, at each stage they take different forms and are reinforced by special forces: forces of greed and, more important, forces generated by collective functional needs" (p. 485).

11. It is unclear how many stages Eckstein proposes, however. He speaks of "a six-stage process" (p. 477), but I can only find five: the "primal polity" (described on pp. 472–476, although on p. 470 Eckstein also terms this the "social polity"); the "politics of primacy" (described on pp. 477–479); the "prophylactic polity" (pp. 479–480); the "polity of interests" (pp. 481–482); and the "polity of incorporation and of incumbency" (pp. 482–484).

12. This is a standard criticism of functionalist explanations, harking back to such explanations' difficulties with the micro–macro problem. It is one thing to claim that a practice satisfies a functional need; it is quite another to claim that all members of the society, including those disadvantaged by the practice, ought therefore to support it.

13. Be it understood that I am speaking of the conceptual foundations of the field, not the massive output of mid-range theories and empirical studies.

14. See Chapter 3.

6

Defining Political Culture

I. Political Culture Has Theoretical Problems

"Political culture" is potentially a powerful, unifying concept of political science. When it was first proposed by Gabriel Almond (1956) and subsequently employed in *The Civic Culture* (Almond and Verba, 1963), the term promised to solve in a scientific, cross-culturally valid way the micro–macro problem: the classic problem of specifying how people affect their political system, and vice versa.[1] "Culture" (and thus political culture) was understood to transcend the individual, but not to the extent that it negated individual action entirely. True, individuals were socialized into their culture, but they also produced and reproduced it. Culture was also understood to constrain political systems, without being identical to them: only certain systems could "fit" a given culture,[2] but the unintended consequences of institutions might alter the culture that created them. The success of anthropologists in studying culture assured political scientists that, properly defined, "political culture" could be studied in all societies.[3] Although formalizing and operationalizing the concept might require new methods, new data, and new theories, the concept itself seemed unproblematic.

Despite its surface simplicity, political culture has presented surprisingly complex conceptual problems. Almond's (1956:396) initial formulation defined political culture as the "particular pattern of orientations to political action." Almond and Verba (1963) revised this conceptualization to the "distribution of patterns of orientation"—a more individual-level conceptualization. Since those formulations were first proposed, many theoretical works have noted problems in defining, measuring, and testing hypotheses in political culture.[4] This stream of criticisms parallels and to some extent overlaps a second stream of new conceptualizations of the concept.[5] These new conceptualizations do not retire older ones; they only jostle them for attention. Such a proliferation of conceptualizations is natural for an important, widely used concept like political culture, but thirty years of conceptualizations and theoretical criticisms have failed to redeem the earlier promise of the concept. Political culture remains a suggestive rather than a scientific concept.[6]

The problem is two-fold: social scientists seek both a consensus on the term's meaning and a redemption of the term's promise. Consensus can be achieved by fiat, by predominant usage, and by analysis. Consensus by fiat is not possible, because social scientists acknowledge no philosophical Leviathan. Even if they did, such a Leviathan would not necessarily create a conceptualization possessing the theoretical characteristics that social scientists expect of it. Consensus by predominant usage is also not possible. Political culture is currently in a state where the leading approach—that of Almond and Verba (1963)—has achieved only a modest plurality and may have done so, moreover, only because of its methodological convenience.[7] In any case, the predominance of a conceptualization does not guarantee its usefulness.

An analytical approach may be able to create both consensus and usefulness, however. This chapter takes such an approach. First, it sets forth nine criteria for conceptualizations of political culture. Analysts of political culture, whether theoreticians or empirical researchers, have long shared common expectations of the concept, despite imperfect satisfaction of those expectations by the analysts' conceptualizations. Even when such expectations have seemed impossible to fulfill, the many critiques of previous conceptualizations have clarified them. The nine criteria should, then, provide a common starting point for evaluating alternative conceptualizations. In addition, if the criteria indeed represent theoretically central problems, their satisfaction should yield a useful conceptualization. Given widespread agreement on theoretically central issues, an analytical approach could create consensus on a conceptualization that redeems political culture's theoretical promise.

Second, this chapter evaluates five major previous conceptualizations against these criteria. Since the problems of studying and theorizing about political culture arise in part from multiple existing conceptualizations, we should examine previous formulations before turning to new ones. None of these earlier conceptualizations satisfies all nine criteria, although Lowell Dittmer's "symbol system" approach is able to satisfy seven of the nine.

Third, looking at social behavior from the perspective of symbolic interactionism, the chapter proposes a new conceptualization of political culture in terms of patterns of meaningful action (ways of relating) that are ambiguously encapsulated in symbols. The proposed conceptualization employs the Piagetian cognitive structure of the patterns to satisfy the two criteria not satisfied by Dittmer's conceptualization, while otherwise retaining its strengths.

Finally, the chapter examines its proposed conceptualization's consequences for research. Data gathering methods change when studying relationships instead of symbols. Since cognitive development does not appear to stop until the individual is well into adulthood, socialization studies must be both greatly extended and refocused to detect cognitive-structural changes. For example, hypotheses about cognitive structure may have to take different forms from those of hypotheses about group distributions of individual orientations, and such hypotheses would have to be tested in a different manner as well.

Following earlier theoretical works, this chapter concentrates on the "culture" portion of the term political culture. "Culture" is the wider concept and so logically must be clarified before the more specific problems of defining "political culture" can be resolved. Accordingly, I adopt a broad view of "the political" until the issues raised here about "culture" are resolved.[8] I will return to this issue in Section VIII.

II. Nine Criteria for Political Culture Conceptualizations

Broadly, the criteria for conceptualizations of political culture arise from three general concerns: a) that political culture offer distinctively new forms of analysis (criteria 1, 2, and 5), particularly those appropriate to the micro–macro problem (1 and 2); b) that the concept not be limited to specific cultures or predicated upon a priori empirical assumptions (criteria 3, 6, and 7); c) and that it be of scientific value (criteria 4, 5, 8, and 9). The specific criteria come from Almond's Parsonian conceptualization of culture[9] (criteria 1, 2, 3, and 5) and from the necessities of comparative politics (criteria 6, 7, and 8) and of social science in general (criteria 4 and 9).[10] Specific justifications for each criterion's validity appear below:

1. *Supramembership*. The conceptualization of culture must distinguish culture from mere aggregates of individuals considered in isolation. As Lehman (1972) insists, culture is a "supramembership" (emergent) property. Kavanagh (1972:63) notes that arguing "from the aggregated features of individuals to the global characteristics [i.e., culture] of a group of which the individuals are members" is the individualistic fallacy (also known as the fallacy of composition). As Dittmer (1977:555) points out, "If political culture can be reduced to the distribution of attitudes among a given population, wherein lies the need for a distinct conceptual framework and line of inquiry?" The very different cultures of the Weimar Republic and the Third Reich both arose from the same German population.

2. *Sharedness*. The conceptualization of culture must refer specifically to something shared among people. The importance and uniqueness of culture lie in its role as a common framework of mutual orientation. In what sense could people have a culture if it were not something shared among them? The response of contextual analysis—that people in the group all equally confront the distribution of characteristics found in that group—will not do: that position makes any arbitrary collection of people a culture.

3. *Inequality*. The conceptualization of culture must allow for the *possibility* that different people have different degrees of influence over the culture. "In reality, the political culture is almost certainly differentially determined by individuals according to their political weight and the intensity behind their particular orientations" (Kavanagh, 1972:61). Such inequality is the raison d'être of studies of elite political culture (e.g., Putnam, 1976). Even if one believes that all actors do have equal influence, directly or indirectly, this should be an empirical conclusion, not a premise built into culture's conceptualization.[11]

4. *Behavioral.* The conceptualization of culture must be such that culture's effects can be observed in social behavior—actions performed when taking other people into account.[12] " Behavior itself gives obvious clues to the sorts of orientations with which [political culture] is associated" (Almond and Powell, 1966:51). Social scientists are interested only in concepts that are at least potentially determinative of observable behavior. This criterion permits nonbehavioral conceptualizations, but by insisting on behavioral consequences it prohibits merely metaphysical abstractions.

5. *Postbehavioral.* The conceptualization must distinguish culture from mere regularities of behavior. Factors other than culture—physical geography springs to mind—can cause regularities of behavior, so even if culture is observed in behavioral regularities, it is not defined by them. Geertz (1973:3–30) terms baldly factual reports of behavior "thin description" in contrast to "thick description," which situates behavior in its web of cultural meaning. (See also the discussions in Lehman, 1972:esp.361–2; Dittmer, 1977:esp.555–556; McAuley, 1984; and Section VII below.) To paraphrase Dittmer's previously cited remark, if political culture can be reduced to empirical regularities of behavior, wherein lies the need for a distinct framework and line of inquiry? Note that this criterion does not contradict the previous one, though satisfaction of both may be difficult.

6. *Unrestricted Applicability.* The conceptualization must apply to the entire range of human social organization, so that social scientists may use the concept without restriction. Conceptualizations of political culture in terms of, say, attitudes toward the military would be meaningless for societies without an institutionalized military or for most forms of social organization smaller than nation-states. (See the discussions in Dittmer, 1977:558ff.; and Scheuch, 1967, 1968.) The point of using a broad concept like culture is to permit our theories the widest possible scope. Empirical variations in social organization may ultimately limit us to "mid-range" theories, but we can never hope for anything greater if our conceptualizations build in limitations.

7. *Nonreductionism.* Beyond wide applicability, the conceptualization must also permit full attention to the unique aspects of any culture's approach to politics. In particular, a conceptualization in terms of some lowest common denominator of all societies would be unsatisfactory, because it would prevent social scientists from comprehending the richness and uniqueness of different cultures (Scheuch, 1967, 1968).

8. *Comparability.* The conceptualization must permit meaningful comparisons of cultures, and within a single society, meaningful comparisons of different facets of its culture. Many important hypotheses implicitly require meaningful cross-cultural comparisons: for example, "Societies with cultural form X have more internal conflict than societies with other cultural forms." Social scientists also need to compare different facets of the culture in order to predict intrasociety dynamics, as in hypotheses like Marx's famous "superstructure" theorem, which relates the culture of economic relations to the

culture of intellectual production; or like Geertz's (1973:452) speculations about the relationship of the Balinese cockfight to the 1965 Balinese "intravillage slaughter."

9. *Objective Testability*. The conceptualization must be capable of producing hypotheses that are testable by objective standards against empirical data. Pye (1972:73–76) notes the current lack of objective standards for testing political-cultural hypotheses. (See also Kavanagh, 1972, and Pateman, 1971.)[13]

We now employ these criteria to assess five conceptualizations of political culture: the classic *Civic Culture* approach; Daniel Elazar's analysis of U. S. subcultures; Kenneth Jowitt's, and Archie Brown's analyses of Marxist-Leninist political culture; and Lowell Dittmer's "symbol system" approach. The next section discusses the first four approaches; the following, Dittmer's approach. These five represent a wide range of approaches. Furthermore, within political science they are also the best-known, the most widely used, and in my judgment the most successful conceptualizations of political culture. If the criteria are useful, they should apply to these five cases; and if political science does in fact have an adequate conceptualization of political culture, it should be found among these.

Because this chapter's primary concern is the evaluation rather than the description of different approaches to political culture, it presents these approaches only to the extent required to assess their satisfaction of the nine criteria. It also evaluates the *conceptualizations* of these earlier approaches, not the value of their research findings. Conceptualizations are not neutral media for conducting researchers' intuition: rather, they are active, if often unrecognized, guides to significant questions and insightful discoveries. In the case of political culture, these significant questions concern the connection, in cross-cultural perspective, of individuals and broader social organization. The nine criteria tell us whether a conceptualization directs or misdirects our research efforts toward those ends. The conceptualizations analyzed below have all produced findings of such scope and suggestiveness as to be ample testimony to their originators' intuition, but our hope is that greater theoretical clarity will lead to deeper insights. It is in this spirit that the theoretical critiques below must be read.

III. Theoretical Evaluation of Previous Conceptualizations

Researchers in the tradition of *The Civic Culture* define political culture as the distribution of aggregated individual characteristics in a population.[14] Research in this tradition typically employs sample surveys. For example, subjects in five countries were asked how they would feel if their sons or daughters were to marry opposition party supporters; the responses show that the five countries differ in the distribution of responses. However, the conceptualization of political culture represented by this approach fails to satisfy criteria 1, 2, 3, and 9: supramembership, sharedness, inequality, and objective testability. It identifies political culture with the aggregate characteristics of individuals, and therefore does not satisfy the supramembership criterion. The only thing social actors "share" in their political culture, according to this conceptualization, is their common existence within a society having the given distribution of individual characteristics.[15] This is the concern of contextual analysis, not political culture: the political culture in the *Civic Culture* formulation is not "shared" in any interpersonal sense, and thus does not satisfy the sharedness criterion. Since each respondent is weighted equally in determining the political culture, it also does not meet the inequality criterion.[16] And because no nonproblematic standards exist for the characterization of political culture, this approach does not fulfill the objective testability criterion (Kavanagh, 1972:56; Pateman, 1971).

In addition, conceptualizations of the type offered in *The Civic Culture* may not satisfy the unrestricted applicability criterion if the individual characteristics studied are not found in all societies. For example, Almond and Verba (1963) studied "attitude toward inter-party marriage," but a party system may not exist in every polity or may have different meanings in different polities.[17] Researchers have no transcendent justification for identifying social objects in different societies with one another. Such methods certainly show that individual, cultural, and social-structural differences exist, but cannot determine whether such differences make any substantial difference to the political process (Scheuch, 1967, 1968). For these and the reasons given in the previous paragraph, the *Civic Culture* conceptualization and others similar to it satisfy only four or five of the nine criteria.

The major competitor to the *Civic Culture* tradition is that begun by Daniel Elazar's (1966, 1970) influential analyses of subcultures in the United States. Elazar identifies three U.S. subcultures: the traditionalistic, the moralistic, and the individualistic. These subcultures dominate different regions of the country, and each has a distinctive set of values, which in turn create a distinctive form of politics.[18]

But despite his description of specific political subcultures, Elazar presents no coherent conceptualization of political culture per se—that is, of what constitutes culture in the abstract. He cites several works—Almond's (1956) conceptualization (Elazar, 1966:84, 1970:256), *The Civic Culture* (Elazar, 1966:85, 1970:258), and various anthropologists and linguists (Elazar, 1970:257)—but he does not appear actually to use their methods. He does not, for example, conduct surveys in the manner of *The Civic Culture* to delineate the beliefs and extent of each culture, although he apparently makes use of surveys collected for other purposes. His *Cities of the Prairie* alternates between regarding political culture as *determined* by the "political style, questions, issues, and processes of the locality" (Elazar,1970:454) and as *defined* by these factors (Elazar,1970:455). While Elazar may be an acute observer of U.S. political orientations, his method is not presented clearly enough to be generalized, and his basic theory of culture is nonexistent.

Elazar's conceptualization does not satisfy at least criteria 6 and 7: unrestricted applicability and nonreductionism. He freely acknowledges (Elazar,1970:280) that his focus on democracy makes his work readily applicable only to the United States. If Elazar really wishes to insist on the connection of his conceptualization to that of *The Civic Culture*, then he imports that work's theoretical problems: criteria 1, 2, 3, and 9. [19] Clearly Elazar knows more than he is telling us, but his focus solely on the United States, and particularly the general ambiguity of his conceptualization, renders it theoretically inadmissible.

Kenneth Jowitt (1974:1173) defines political culture as "the informal organization of the state . . . the set of informal, adaptive postures—behavioral and attitudinal—that emerge in response to and interact with the set of formal definitions—ideological, policy, and institutional—that characterize a given level of society." This conceptualization leads into a fascinating interpretive analysis of the problems faced by Communist regimes in attempting to replace the pre-existing political culture with a Marxist-Leninist one.

Jowitt's conceptualization has an unusual combination of strengths and weaknesses. Unlike Elazar, Jowitt rightly excludes social structure from culture by differentiating formal rules and informal adaptations. However, Jowitt confuses a *hypothesis* about the relationship of regime and culture with a *conceptualization* of the latter when he assumes that political culture arises and exists only as an adaptation to a regime. How culture originates and whether it is the cause or effect of regime structure are empirical issues.

We can, however, ignore the issue of how the adaptations arise and simply look at what sort of sociological object they are. From this perspective, Jowitt's conceptualization may satisfy the supramembership criterion, although Jowitt does not clearly specify how "informal, adaptive postures" are to be measured. Jowitt's conceptualization probably does not satisfy the sharedness criterion, however, because there is no guarantee that responses to a regime will be shared. Like the *Civic Culture*'s "orientations," responses to a regime may be quite diverse.

Jowitt's conceptualization clearly satisfies criteria 3, 4, and 5. His conceptualization of culture as the response to a regime clearly sees culture as manipulable to some extent by the regime, and thus satisfies the inequality criterion. Jowitt discusses at length the response to a regime evidenced in adaptive behavior; the conceptualization thus meets the behavioral criterion. The postbehavioral criterion is met because Jowitt defines culture as a set of postures guiding action, not as the action itself.

The conceptualization satisfies criterion 6 (unrestricted applicability) only if we are willing to assume that every society has, in Jowitt's words, a "set of formal definitions—ideological, policy, and institutional." This assumption is valid for nation-states, the objects of Jowitt's research, but it is less plausible for tribal societies, for example, and is implausible for small, nongovernmental institutions like families or small groups. Perhaps Jowitt could clarify the concept of "formal definitions" to permit its application to such cases, but the point is strained. In any event, Jowitt does not argue it.

Within these constraints, however, the conceptualization does seem to satisfy criterion 7 (nonreductionism), because it permits free exploration of each society's unique adaptations.

Finally, the conceptualization does not satisfy either the objective testability or comparability criterion. Like the *Civic Culture* conceptualization and others similar to it, Jowitt's conceptualization is not readily susceptible to objective standards of hypothesis-testing that uses objective data. In addition, the conceptualization is global and intuitive, making comparisons of cultures difficult. Jowitt's conceptualization must therefore also be judged inadmissible.

Archie Brown's (1977:1) conceptualization of political culture includes a potpourri of social elements: "the subjective perception of history and politics, the fundamental beliefs and values, the foci of identification and loyalty, and the political knowledge and expectations which are the product of the specific historical experiences of nations and groups." As with Jowitt's complex definition, this combination of elements produces at once both strength and weakness. The strength of Brown's conceptualization arises from its deliberate demarcation of a set of interesting elements to study. Far more than a conceptualization, Brown's phrase carries an entire implicit theory: of where culture comes from ("historical experiences of nations and groups"); of its manifestation in shared group symbols ("foci of identification and loyalty"); and of its manifestation in individuals ("subjective perceptions" and "fundamental beliefs and values"). In consequence, Brown's approach has led to a variety of suggestive empirical results (e.g., Brown and Gray, 1977).

This strength is, however, also the source of theoretical weakness. It is one thing to catalogue the concomitants of political culture; it is quite another to define it. By calling his phrase a conceptualization, Brown conflates individual ("subjective") perceptions and group symbols ("foci of identification and loyalty"). As the discussion of *The Civic Culture* in preceding pages and in Sections IV and V of this chapter makes clear, these are distinct social elements, which satisfy different subsets of the nine criteria. To the theorist, the conjoining of these elements—*in the absence of further conceptual integration of their disparate aspects*—results in a combination of their separate weaknesses, not their strengths. Just as we saw when examining the *Civic Culture* conceptualization, which Brown's closely resembles, this aspect of his conceptualization prevents it from satisfying criteria 1, 2, 3, and 9, and possibly 7.

As a rough and ready guide to political culture's theoretical environment, Brown's phrase has been empirically productive. As a conceptualization of political culture, however, the phrase requires additional coordination of its separate elements. We shall see below, however, that certain portions of Brown's phrase are very close to the conceptualization advanced in this chapter.

IV. Lowell Dittmer's Conceptualization: Political Culture as Symbol System

Lowell Dittmer (1977:566) defines political culture as "a system of political symbols, and this system nests within a more inclusive system that we might term 'political communication.'" This conceptualization turns sharply away from the weakness of individual-centered conceptualizations like Almond and Verba's, and yet does not rely on the presence or absence of (nonuniversal) political institutions. The conceptualization accordingly differs from previous conceptualizations in satisfying all but the last two theoretical criteria.

The conceptualization satisfies the supramembership criterion because the symbols of political discourse are used in communication, which by definition goes beyond the individual. It fulfills the sharedness criterion to the extent that these symbols have common meaning. Dittmer does not explore what becomes of the nature or status of a symbol if, as some studies show,[20] it means different things to different people. But note that the conceptualization's problem with sharedness is different from that of *The Civic Culture*, which makes the distribution of differences the very centerpiece of its conceptualization. Dittmer hopes his symbols are shared, but can't prove they are; in *The Civic Culture*, the issue is irrelevant.

A long research tradition discusses how people have, or might have, differential degrees of control over the meaning and use of symbols;[21] accordingly, Dittmer's conceptualization meets the inequality criterion. Dittmer's conceptualization also satisfies the behavioral criterion, since people's symbolically mediated understanding of the political world determines in part their political behavior (Hewitt, 1979). Moreover, although symbols affect behavior, they are not identical with it: they are neither defined in terms of it, nor a perfect empirical determinant of it. Thus Dittmer's conceptualization also meets the postbehavioral criterion.

Symbols appear to have similar functions in all societies.[22] Therefore, as long as social scientists do not restrict themselves to any particular medium of communication or class of symbols, Dittmer's conceptualization satisfies the unrestricted applicability criterion.

Each culture deals uniquely with the objective conditions it faces, and this uniqueness is expressed in its symbols. Symbolic meaning within the culture must be accurately understood, of course: researchers must not use an ethnocentric interpretive framework to establish meanings. Assuming this caveat is heeded, the study of culture in terms of symbols does justice to the uniqueness of each culture, and Dittmer's conceptualization meets the criterion of nonreductionism.

Dittmer's conceptualization has difficulty satisfying the comparability criterion, however. Cross-cultural comparison of symbols is difficult, because every symbol is meaningful only within a larger symbol system or subsystem of the culture (Geertz, 1973). Intercultural comparisons consequently require the comparison of entire symbol systems (or subsystems), not individual symbols;

and, as has sometimes been the case in past national character studies, social scientists are reduced to comparing these systems/subsystems through intuitive global judgments. A similar problem arises in assessing the *internal* coherence of a culture by comparing symbol subsystems.

Global characterizations of culture allow cross-cultural testing only if culture-free dimensions of comparison can be found. Such culture-free dimensions are notoriously scarce. Global characterization also offers no way to test whether specific aspects of the symbol system are consonant with the global characterization. For example, Pye (1972:294) asks, referring to Clifford Geertz's (1973) description of the Balinese cockfight, what is the "relationship between the important place that cockfighting occupies in Balinese culture and the violent intra-village slaughtering of Balinese [by] each other after the unsuccessful Communist coup of 1965"? It is "plausible" that the two are related, as Pye notes, but social scientists desire a more objective criterion than plausibility. Therefore, Dittmer's conceptualization does not meet the objective testability criterion.

Despite its failure to meet the two last criteria, Dittmer's approach marks a considerable theoretical advance. As we shall see below, its problems with comparability and objective testability turn out to be resolvable through a little theoretical finesse involving the cognitive structure of symbol systems. Conceptualizations such as the one elaborated in *The Civic Culture*, on the other hand, remain trapped in a morass of problems arising from their individual-level origins. It may be that these latter formulations can be resuscitated somehow, but I can see no way of doing so. The remainder of this chapter is therefore concerned solely with showing how, by transforming Dittmer's conceptualization into a slightly different framework, its advantages can be preserved and its disadvantages overcome, resulting in a fully admissible conceptualization.

V.   Political Culture as Publicly Common Ways of Relating

The participants in the Aspen Institute conference worried this question [of why, when everyone knows that torture was being conducted, there was still a need to take the political risk involved in making that knowledge explicit] around the table several times—the necessary distinctions seemed particularly slippery and elusive— and then Thomas Nagel, a professor of philosophy and law at New York University, stumbled upon an answer. "It's the differences between knowledge and *ac*knowledgement," Nagel said haltingly. "It's what happens and can only happen to knowledge when it becomes officially sanctioned, when it is made part of the *public* cognitive scene." Yes, several of the panelists agreed. And that transformation, another participant added, is sacramental (Weschler, 1989:43).

Every cultural symbol stands for, justifies, describes, or otherwise contemplates a culture's "way of relating"—the organized system of mutual expectations by which social behavior is informed and made meaningful.[23] Different actors may attach different meanings to the symbol, but their references are all to ways of relating. A little later I will discuss the implications of the possible conflict between interpretations; for now, let us examine one well-known symbol—the U.S. flag—in order to pursue the connection between symbols and ways of relating.

The U.S. flag signals an area where people relate to one another in a special way. Flown in a VFW Hall, it signals the dominance of intensely patriotic ways of relating. Flown elsewhere, the flag may signal the dominance of particular official ways of relating: e.g., the relations constituting a military post, city government, or other specially regulated institutions. In all these cases the flag indicates not so much a physical as a social territory: a region where certain social relations obtain. The decoding of a cultural symbol is simply the elucidation of these implied social relations.

Such decoding is necessary, of course, to eliminate the ambiguity of the symbol: two citizens can both wear American flag lapel pins and still come to blows over political differences. If symbols had one meaning, social scientists would not have to interpret them and politicians could not fight over them. Ways of relating thus seem to constitute a prior, more exact level of analysis than symbols.[24]

How people relate to one another is both the general subject of empirical social science (how *do* people relate to one another) and the central concern of normative social theory (how *should* they relate to one another). We are thus fascinated by Geertz's (1973) description of the Balinese cockfight in the context of Balinese village life only incidentally because it describes strange and interesting practices, but more important because it reveals how the Balinese relate to one another. The cockfights do not just symbolize how the Balinese relate; they *are* a relationship. If Geertz had simply viewed the cockfight as a symbol of Balinese life, or had described the Balinese "beliefs, attitudes, and values" concerning the cockfight, he would have led his readers away from the cockfight's immediate significance as one of the media through which the Balinese relate to one another. It is Geertz's description of this way of relating *as* a way of relating that makes it of such theoretical interest and, not by accident, human interest.

Given this central concern with ways of relating, and given the (one-to-many) correspondence between symbols and ways of relating, this chapter recasts Dittmer's conceptualization of political culture in terms of ways of relating. This recasting does not deny the importance of symbols, which Dittmer has already shown, but rather points more exactly to the nature of their importance. Symbols are an intermediate level of analysis, indicating what ways of relating the culture (or the observer) finds important enough to encapsulate in symbolic form. To conceive culture in terms of ways of relating rather than symbols is therefore to go more directly to the object of interest. In addition, even though all ways of relating are of potential interest to social scientists, do we know that all are represented symbolically? If some ways of relating are not symbolized, as seems likely, then "ways of relating" defines more accurately than "symbol systems" the field of inquiry.

Let us define culture in terms of ways of relating. I first propose to call "a culture" *only* groups of people who share, in the special way described below, a way of relating. Note that this "bottom-up" approach is opposite to earlier, "top-down" approaches. These latter approaches take collectivities (e.g., countries) a priori, term them cultures, and examine afterwards whether their members have anything in common. The present approach looks for commonality before bestowing the name "culture" on a collectivity.

I next propose to term a way of relating "shared" only if it is *publicly common* within the collectivity. "Publicly common" means that the way of relating is both (a) understood by all in the culture (a *common* understanding); and (b) in fact used by all actors to orient to one another (the *public* focus of orientation).[25] It follows that a large, diverse collectivity may well have *no* political culture—may, properly speaking, not be a political culture. The concept of public commonness—the actual *use* of a way of relating—makes analysts more aware of who does and who does not "participate in the culture." Even in such a highly selective and self-conscious institution as Congress, for example, certain members exhibit inappropriate behavior. Social science must differentiate a Congresswoman's strategic power, available to all 535 members, from participation in Congress' dominant culture, which may be shared by only 534, or 533, etc. Nothing guarantees that any given agglomeration of people will have a culture.

The insistence on public commonness is necessary for four theoretical reasons. First, it eliminates ad hoc specifications of which social aggregates are cultures. Social scientists loosely term the United States a culture, but what criterion beyond our own judgment shows that it is? *The Civic Culture* finds quite disparate views in the United States: by what right do researchers assume this diversity to be one culture? Researchers have justifications only truculent ("Because I *say* it's a culture"), tautological ("Because it's all the United States"), or question-begging ("Because it has one government"). The public commonness restriction insists that a culture extends only so far as people choose the same way to relate to one another, which seems to be the unity referred to when we say people "participate in" a culture.

Second, the public commonness restriction allows cultures to be studied and characterized as wholes, because by definition all actors in the culture work within shared, and acted-upon, ways of relating. The analyst can reintroduce the natural complexity of a mixed society through concepts of subculture and cultural conflict, while allowing analytic power to be applied to truly homogeneous cultures.

Third, the insistence upon publicness distinguishes acquiescence from approval, acknowledging that cultural expectations can differ from individuals' preferred ways of relating. This distinction frees the conceptualization of political culture from Talcott Parsons's much-criticized faith in value consensus. "When in Rome, do as the Romans do" could be the official motto of political culture: one might like to deal with people in a certain way, but prior, publicly common expectations constrain one's behavior. The existence of a political culture is not defined by the condition of all people liking the culture or regarding it as legitimate. Rather, it is defined by the ways of relating that people actually use to coordinate their dealings with one another. Culture is what is publicly expected and subscribed to, not what is individually preferred.

Consider race relations in the United States before and after the intense civil rights movement of the 1950s and 1960s. Clearly, U.S. society now deals with racial issues far differently than it did in the past: race relations have been irreversibly altered, even if private attitudes have in many cases remained unchanged. The rapid evolution and political achievements of the civil rights movement reflected not a sudden change of heart by millions of U.S. citizens but rather the mobilization of people already dissatisfied with existing race relations. Surveys tell us that individual attitudes about racial issues have gradually become more liberal, but the standard expectations of how to relate to different races changed suddenly. Individual preferences obviously influence what ways of relating can become publicly common, and the nature of such influence is of much interest to us, but individual preference and public commonness are logically distinct.

This distinction is the theoretical port of entry for considerations of social power. Culture is established and maintained not just from people's preferences (and moral reasoning, as I argue later) but also from their relative ability to make those preferences publicly common. This is the domain of economic control, military power, media access, and all the other powers through which a relatively unpopular way of relating might become the focus of orientation.

Fourth, considerations of public commonness underlie two important social phenomena: socialization and cultural change. Public commonness is difficult to maintain, and this difficulty is responsible for society's immense investment of labor in schooling and other methods of socialization. Public commonness is also difficult to establish and alter. Immense social upheavals are required for cultural change, perhaps not initially while new ways of relating gradually become common, but certainly later while they become publicly common. Researchers can understand fully neither socialization nor social change without adducing the concept of public commonness.

Although the insistence on public commonness is necessary for the above reasons, will there be any new costs from this insistence? One such cost might be that culture can be determined only ex post facto and provisionally. Cultures can shift rapidly as people adopt (or fall away from) an existing publicly common way of relating. This is, however, only a practical nuisance to the researcher, not a theoretical drawback. Indeed, everyday observation regularly confirms that people drop in and out of social movements. The occasional bumps of social life show us that people cannot be certain that others share their orientation. The above point is then not a cost of the proposed conceptualization but evidence that it captures an ordinary circumstance of social life.

A second apparent cost of the conceptualization is that societies are no longer seen as coherent cultures. Emphasis on the establishment of public commonness and on the choices people make among competing ways of relating—does this not focus our attention unduly on conflict rather than consensus? I think, however, that it is more accurate to say that once one does not *assume* consensus, one recognizes the *possibility* of conflict. The conceptualization requires a focus neither on consensus nor on conflict, but rather allows the researcher to study their presence without preconceptions. And it does seem, furthermore, that the nature of conflict contemplated by the conceptualization—conflict over general ways of relating to one another—is of immense social importance. (For example, such conflict is central to the dynamics of political development.) The apparent cost to researchers of a loss of coherence is in fact a gain in the sensitivity and importance of the resulting analyses.

VI.   The Proposed Conceptualization Satisfies Criteria 1–7

The conceptualization of political culture as "all publicly common ways of relating within the collectivity" satisfies the supramembership criterion, because the public commonness of a way of relating is not a characteristic of the individual (or of arbitrarily aggregated individuals). One cannot determine if a culture exists by examining individuals in isolation. The conceptualization satisfies tautologically the sharedness criterion, because in this understanding a culture is said to exist only insofar as its ways of relating are publicly common— i.e., shared.

In this sense the *Civic Culture*'s participant, subject, and parochial orientations may be the basis of actual cultures, but their associated ways of relating must be identified. Even if identified, it is still unclear whether the participant and subject cultures together make a new "civic culture," because the authors do not show on what common basis they can relate to one another. Carole Pateman (1971, 1980), in particular, wants very much to know how "participants" relate to "subjects," because this relationship will evidence such class domination as exists, and she criticizes the *Civic Culture* and similar conceptualizations for their neglect of that relationship.

The proposed conceptualization fulfills the inequality criterion, because it does not assume that social actors have equal ability to establish public commonness. One can at least imagine the possibility that differentials of power could give social actors differential control over what way of relating is publicly common.[26] The present conceptualization assumes neither equality nor inequality, but simply points to the empirical issue of how public commonness is established and maintained.

The proposed conceptualization obviously meets the behavioral criterion, because the definition of any social situation makes some behaviors more appropriate than others. The way people define situations, and the effect of those definitions on behavior, constitute the subject matter of symbolic interactionism.[27]

Because not all empirical regularities of behavior arise from ways of relating, the conceptualization also meets the postbehavioral criterion. For example, travelers crossing the desert stop at water holes not out of shared culture but out of physical necessity. Nor do empirical regularities of social behavior always show the presence of a culture. A person who obeys the law because a policeman is standing nearby does not have the same way of relating as a person who obeys the law because it is sacred. The behaviors of the two may resemble one another in some circumstances, but they share no broad cultural basis for behavior.

Just as all cultures have symbols, all cultures have ways of relating, and the concept of ways of relating is naturally applicable cross-culturally. Thus the proposed conceptualization fulfills the unrestricted applicability criterion.

And just as symbols express the uniqueness of a culture, so ways of relating express that uniqueness. Symbols such as the flag or the name "U.S.A." represent distinctions, made within the cultural ways of relating, by which the culture demarcates itself. Symbols encapsulate the way of relating: indeed, to explain the way of relating often requires reference to the symbols.[28] Thus the proposed conceptualization satisfies the nonreductionism criterion.

We have not yet discussed the comparability and objective testability criteria. The concept of "ways of relating" recognizes culture's richness but not what is comparable between cultures. If no cross-culturally valid characterization of cultures is available, then social scientists cannot test hypotheses of intercultural regularities. If cultural ways of relating can only be characterized as wholes, then each configuration merely receives a different name, and social scientists cannot test hypotheses of intracultural coherence.

The following sections argue that these problems with comparability and testability can be overcome by recognizing that ways of relating are constituted in reasoning, which has Piagetian cognitive structure,[29] and which therefore can be analyzed in the powerful ways unique to cognitive structure. Note that our pursuit of political culture has led us first to symbols, then to the ways of relating "underneath" symbols, and now to the reasoning structures "underneath" ways of relating. Here the analysis touches bottom, in the form of solid empirical work, but the reader must be aware that a new level is being discussed.

VII.   Ways of Relating have Moral Reasoning Structure

The term "ways of relating" has a nice behavioral ring to it, raising images of objective, observable patterns of behavior. Such images must be rejected, however.[30] Social behavior comes not out of fixed behavior patterns but rather as people engage social situations by interpreting them. People identify, interconnect, and consequently make meaningful their own and others' actions. Whether their reasoning involves simple actions or complex internalized representations of action, it remains reasoning. Ordinary discourse recognizes such a preliminary process organizing action: we ask people how they see things, why they did that, and how they came to that conclusion, and we expect a coherent response.[31]

Fixed environments may induce recurrent responses, but environmental changes quickly reveal these responses' foundation in reasoning. Some people believe, for example, that bureaucratic behavior arises solely from following regular, mindless bureaucratic procedures. But as any bureaucrat can attest, even obedient clients can present problems calling for interpretation. Moreover, as Danet (1971) points out, some clients also use extralegal appeals: sob stories, bribes, and even threats. Such appeals require the bureaucrat to re-reason her use of the rule book by asking, "What is the value of following the rules when set against (e.g.,) a monetary gain for myself?" The answer may be obvious to the reader, but the long history of bureaucratic corruption shows it is not inevitably obvious to bureaucrats. In short, any way of relating, including that represented by the most structured bureaucracy, is founded on reasoning rather than fixed rules. Researchers must, therefore, inquire into people's understandings of their behavior, not the behavior alone.

Reasoning about one's social behavior is ipso facto moral reasoning, because it shows how one takes the claims of others into account—what claims, in what way, and to what extent. When one decides how to behave in relation to others, one is of necessity making a moral judgment. This is true even of relations like ethnicity or gender, which appear based in biology rather than moral reasoning. Such relations are cultural constructions. For example, in New Mexico I would be one of an undifferentiated group of "Anglos." In Minnesota, however, I am not "Anglo" but "Norwegian"—and hence the ancient foe of the "Swedes." My ethnic status and consequent relationships are thus not so much biological facts as they are the moral expectations of my cultural surroundings regarding how I am to identify and treat other people. Cultural constructions like ethnicity and gender are so pervasive that it is easy to forget their basis in moral reasoning.

An extensive body of longitudinal, cross-cultural, and cross-sectional research has shown that moral reasoning has Piagetian cognitive structure. The following claims, all supported by that research, are relevant to the present argument:[32]

1. Moral reasoning varies in its structure (the logical interrelationships of the concepts). There are six possible structures, called "stages."[33]
2. The stages can be hierarchically ordered such that each stage represents a differentiation and coordination of the previous stage (Kohlberg, 1981, 1984a; Kohlberg, Levine, and Hewer, 1984a).[34]
3. Stages are acquired in hierarchical order, with no skipping of stages and no retrogression to lower stages (Colby et al., 1983).
4. Progression through the stages depends initially on the successive recognition of the relativity of each stage to different moral concerns and

perspectives and ultimately on an appropriate reorganization of that stage to embrace and coordinate those perspectives. Thus progression is not inevitable, but it is possible—for any person, at any stage, whenever she perceives such relativity (Kohlberg, 1981, 1984a).

5. The above statements apply uniformly to all societies (Kohlberg, 1981; Kohlberg, Levine, and Hewer, 1984a; Nisan and Kohlberg, 1984; Snarey, Reimer, and Kohlberg, 1984; Weinreich 1977, Edwards, 1975).[35]

The research can support these strong claims because it studies the structure of moral reasoning, not the content. For example, one stage of moral reasoning (called "Stage 3" in Kohlberg's work) involves a "Golden Rule" maintenance of interpersonal relations through mutual role-taking. Consider the following two hypothetical Stage 3 answers to the question of whether a judge should give jail terms to conscientious objectors:

"The judge should put them in jail because that's what's expected of judges."

"The judge should put herself in the conscientious objector's place and have a heart."

In both answers the reasoning is structured in terms of the maintenance of good interpersonal relations and mutual role-taking. The first answer tells the judge to take the role of other members of society, while the second answer tells her to take the role of the accused. The role-taking perspective is ambiguous in its application, and the diversity of content thus stems from the ambiguity of the cognitive structure. If a reasoner were equally sympathetic to both relationships, the apparently major content difference could arise from small, even accidental shifts in the way the issue is presented. This distinction between content and structure is especially important in cross-cultural work, where content differences are extreme.[36]

VIII.   Measurement Techniques

Cognitive psychologists have several standard ways to measure cognitive structure. In Piaget's *méthode clinique,* the subject is given some task requiring cognitive operations, and the researcher alters the task and/or questions the subject to determine the latter's understanding of what she is doing. This method has two practical drawbacks. First, even though Piaget used the method to excellent effect, the lack of a fixed questionnaire makes the method's success entirely dependent on the skill and theoretical grasp of the researcher. Second, the method requires interviews or controlled observations, which are unfeasible in much historical or social science research.

Kohlberg overcomes the first of these problems, though not the second, by using a standard set of moral dilemma stories (e.g., should a poor husband steal a drug necessary to save his wife's life) and follow-up probes (e.g., "What if the husband didn't love his wife?") to elicit his subjects' moral reasoning. The researcher can interview subjects individually, or can administer the stories as a group written test. The responses are scored according to a detailed manual.[37] The method's coverage of the various universal "issues" and "aspects" of moral judgment permits both Kohlberg's test and scoring system to be applied systematically to any culture. (See, for example, Nisan and Kohlberg, 1984, and the references therein; and Snarey, Reimer, and Kohlberg, 1984.)

This scoring system can also be applied to materials other than Kohlberg's standard moral judgment interview. Moral reasoning appears in many forms— inaugural addresses, letters, etc.—and can be scored wherever it appears. (Scoring reliability will vary inversely with the explicitness and extensiveness of the available material.) This permits social scientists and historians to conduct analyses of cognitive structure without interviewing their subjects.

While the above methods measure the moral reasoning of individuals, the present discussion concerns cultural moral reasoning, which is publicly common. In particular, people must use cultural reasoning to communicate with and persuade each other in the context of their culture. As survey researchers know well, one must observe special precautions to get people to respond *outside* their cultural constraints—that is, to speak from the position of their individual preferences instead of from their understanding of what expressions are "in order." Cultural reasoning is the rule, not the exception. Students of culture therefore enjoy at least one advantage: cultural reasoning is easy to obtain. Cultural materials containing such reasoning are already the subject of social-scientific (albeit generally not cognitive-structural) study. To mention only a few examples, social scientists have studied presidential inaugural addresses (Yeager, 1974) and press conferences (McMillian and Ragan, 1983), strike demands (Shorter and Tilly, 1974), theological arguments (Radding, 1979), children's stories (McClelland, 1976), congressional speeches (Rosenwasser, 1969), television shows (Lichter and Lichter, 1983), introductory college textbooks (Bertilson, Springer, and Fierke, 1982), public prayers (Medhurst, 1977), advertisements (Williamson, 1978), editorials (Sinclair, 1982), and newspaper stories (Van Dijk, 1983). Each of these materials contains cultural moral reasoning insofar as it attempts to persuade the audience of, or explain to it, a desired course of action. Only the application of cognitive-structural analysis to these materials would be at all unusual.[38]

Researchers may also elicit cultural moral reasoning experimentally by interviewing respondents in a public setting. Respondents could be asked to write persuasive appeals to other members of their culture. Or, respondents could be asked to study issues, meet in small groups, and decide as a group on the best argument for a course of action. Respondents could be interviewed about the reasoning behind their choices in Prisoner's Dilemma games. Respondents could be interviewed about their moral reasoning in front of their peers.[39] In general, cultural reasoning is easier to study than private reasoning because the researcher can cast aside the classical experimental strictures to isolate the respondent. After all, if a respondent alters her responses when in the company of others, this indicates something about the group's conduct of politics in other settings.

Let me return briefly to the issue raised at the end of Section I: the distinction between political culture and culture broadly understood. If ways of relating are grounded in moral reasoning, then we must look to the nature of morality itself to make our distinctions. This is particularly true for the development and application of cross-cultural analytic concepts, since the distinctions between the political and (e.g.,) economic spheres are made in different ways in different societies. It may be true that the morality of the marketplace will differ from that of the public forum, and if so, the proposed conceptualization of culture will break cleanly into "political culture" and (e.g.,) "economic culture." But if such distinctions are built into our conceptualization a priori, they may easily not have cultural universality and thus may not be theoretically helpful.

The major difficulty in cultural research will be identifying the intended audience, i.e., delineating the specific cultural context within which the materials or responses in question are produced. In their inaugural addresses, whom are our presidents addressing? Their campaign staffs? Campaign contributors? People who had voted for them? Those who hadn't voted for them? Members of their parties? The nation as a whole? All human beings? Since the way of relating chosen will vary with the situation, the researcher must identify which culture is operative. If the researcher is interviewing people directly, she can easily find out how subjects see their imagined (or actual) audience. This task will be more difficult with historical records and, more generally, all expressions where the researcher cannot question the participants. These problems are only methodological, however; they do not affect the validity of the theoretical formulation. The major theoretical claim of this section is simply that culture as defined here is *in principle* measurable, as required by the behavioral criterion. Where researchers can question people directly, such measurement should also be quite straightforward in practice.

IX. The Proposed Conceptualization Satisfies Criteria 8 and 9

This chapter started by noting the proliferation of political culture conceptualizations and has worked its way around to proposing another. The burden of proof is accordingly on the new conceptualization to demonstrate marked advantages. Both Dittmer's and the present conceptualization satisfy criteria 1–7; however, Dittmer's does not offer a ready way to satisfy criteria 8 and 9, comparability and objective testability. This section shows that the proposed conceptualization does satisfy those last two criteria.

We have established that (1) each culture consists of publicly common ways of relating; (2) the ways of relating are constituted in the reasoning that people use to apply them; (3) this reasoning is moral; (4) moral reasoning has cognitive structure; and (5) cognitive structure can be meaningfully compared between different cultures. The cognitive-structural analysis of culture is then meaningful cross-culturally. Moreover, cognitive structure is an important characteristic to study. In a very real sense, one cannot study a culture at all until one has come to grips with the cognitive structure ordering it. The cultural content is important, of course, but it is not independent of the framework of the culture's cognitive structure (Geertz, 1973:3–30).

The extraction of structure from content shows social scientists what is comparable across cultures. Structural statements do not, however, describe specific cultural content. In the example of the judge who must sentence conscientious objectors, a structural analysis of a Stage 3 culture would reveal that actors resolve this moral dilemma in terms of mutual role-taking and maintenance of good interpersonal relations. The structural analysis by itself could not say whose role social actors would take or which interpersonal relationship they would maintain.

This content ambiguity means that cognitive-structural factors do not directly predict behavior. Such factors are far from useless in explanation, however. First, social scientists have already correlated cognitive stage with a variety of behaviors, e.g., altruistic behavior. (See Blasi, 1980 for a review of pre-1980 research, and Candee and Kohlberg, 1983, 1984 for two later examples.) Second, beyond predicting behavior, cognitive stage can serve more usefully as a control variable. The different reasoning structures are qualitatively different, and so causal connections between variables may differ greatly between cognitive stage groups. For example, the maintenance of reciprocal, ideal relationships is the major element of Stage 3 judgments of interpersonal obligations but is irrelevant to earlier stages. Thus a researcher relating, say, marital expectations and education would be well advised to control for cognitive stage in the statistical analysis. Regrettably, most current behavioral studies neglect reasoning structure, combine incommensurable elements, and thus wastefully weaken their results.

Content differences are meaningless until structural differences are understood. Cognitive-structural analysis offers one means of cross-cultural comparison, and the comparability criterion is to that extent satisfied. Content differences between cultures remain to be explained, of course, but such explanations are logically subsequent to structural analysis. Empirical research into culture will remain confused until social scientists control for cognitive-structural differences.

Pye and other theorists have noted the peculiar nature of the explanatory potential of political culture. When reinterpreted in cognitive-structural terms, political culture hypotheses become more straightforward. Hypotheses of intracultural coherence (i.e., that a political culture is unified in its many facets) become claims of cognitive-structural consistency (i.e., that the political culture has the same cognitive structure in all facets). One such hypothesis is advanced by Pye (1972:294) when he posits a "relationship between the important place that cockfighting occupies in Balinese culture and the violent intra-village slaughtering of Balinese [by] each other after the unsuccessful Communist coup of 1965." Rewritten in cognitive-structural terms, the hypothesis is that the culture of the cockfight and the culture of the slaughter have the same underlying cognitive structure. Pye names the explanatory connection "plausibility," but in the structural interpretation it is the more objective "cognitive-structural iso-morphism." The sense of plausibility comes from perceiving the basic cognitive-structural unity present.

The concept of cognitive-structural explanation also clarifies Geertz's statement:

> This is not to say, of course, that the killings were caused by the cockfight, could have been predicted on the basis of it, or were some sort of enlarged version of it with real people in the place of the cocks—all of which is nonsense. It is merely to say that if one looks at Bali . . . —as the Balinese themselves do— . . . through the medium of its cockfight, the fact that the massacre occurred seems, if no less appalling, less like a contradiction to the laws of nature (Geertz, 1973:452).

In cognitive-structural terms, the killings were not caused by the cockfights, because the connection is not one of agency but of structural isomorphism. The killings also could not be predicted on the basis of the cockfights, because structure does not determine content. Thus the killings were not merely an enlarged version of the cockfights: structural isomorphism does not imply content similarity.

Instead, the cognitive-structural explanation connects events in its assumption that people who operate at a given cognitive stage will evince its structure in many aspects of their lives. Such an explanation rarely predicts specific behavior, but it does limit the potential range of behavior exhibited in a culture. Consider the cognitive structure underlying Kohlberg's Stage 3. This structure consists of the mutual maintenance, through reciprocal role-taking, of an ideal relationship between two parties. Moral decisions, and the behavior they impel, are limited to a choice of which pair-relationship one seeks to maintain, without consideration of the wider social consequences of such particularistic concerns. (The specific nature of the relationship being maintained could vary from culture to culture or even situation to situation. Friendship, godparenting, certain patron-client relationships, and late-feudal fealty all have this structure, despite their different contents.) Lehman can be read as referring to the limitations imposed by these cognitive levels when he argues that cultural variables are "specifying variables":

> A specifying variable has only a "modified" explanatory impact, i.e., it "specifies" the conditions under which more strategic correlations will exist in greater or lesser

intensity. Seen in this light, culture should be viewed as one of the conditions of the broader "context" that encourage or inhibit the interaction of social system properties (Lehman, 1972:368).

Cognitive-structural analysis can generate hypotheses of intercultural comparison as well as hypotheses of intracultural coherence. The historian Charles Radding, for example, has argued directly that cognitive-structural changes caused the decline of the medieval ordeal (Radding, 1979) and had more general effects on medieval society (Radding, 1978). The anthropologist C. R. Hallpike (1979) discusses directly the role of cognitive structure in the cultural forms of primitive societies. I personally believe that patron–client systems only appear in Stage 2 (and, in a different form, in Stage 3) cultures. Whether true or not, these hypotheses refer to specific, measurable variables. They can be tested and evaluated by standard statistical methods, thus demonstrating that the proposed conceptualization satisfies the ninth and last criterion of objective testability.

X.   Conclusion

This chapter's argument has three steps. First, it advances nine criteria in terms of which social scientists can evaluate alternative conceptualizations of political culture. The criteria arise from earlier, well-known theoretical critiques and from standard canons of social research. Though the list of criteria can be disputed, the use of a list permits rational discourse about adding or removing specific criteria.

Second, the chapter examines five major current conceptualizations of political culture and finds them subject to various theoretical objections. Of course, this critique of conceptualizations does not necessarily invalidate the previous research findings. The critique questions how the studies relate to political culture, but it does not attack the accuracy or importance of their results.

Third, the chapter proposes a conceptualization claimed to satisfy all nine theoretical criteria. The proposed conceptualization's use of cognitive-structural analysis requires special forms of hypotheses and hypothesis-testing. In particular, the distinction between content and structure alters the way social scientists conceive of cross-cultural comparability: researchers must compare structures first, and contents only among identical structures.

The proposed conceptualization currently lacks two elements: a means of handling content differences, and empirical illustrations. The distinction between content and structure is important and natural, but, clearly, social science cannot rest with purely structural analysis. Ultimately, after due attention is given to the distribution, development, and measurement of various structures, social scientists will still wish to compare the actual contents being structured. The proposed conceptualization of political culture may be only a way station on the route to that complete analysis, but it is a necessary way station: social science cannot develop a clear theory of content until it comes to grips with the structures, which give contents meaning.

The argument for the proposed conceptualization is mainly theoretical: while a clear conceptualization will usually produce clear and insightful results, and certainly Kohlberg's studies have produced such results for individuals, this conceptualization still requires an empirical demonstration of its fruitfulness. In particular, to understand either publicly common ways of relating or their cognitive structure, social scientists must undertake three projects. First, we must develop and validate methods, like those suggested above, for studying cultures, especially their cognitive structures.

Second, we must apply these methods to current and past societies to draw a rudimentary cultural map of the world.[40] Such analyses would differ from (most) current studies in that they would focus on cognitive stages. Different cultures will be organized in different cognitive structures, and the stage theory offers what promises to be a useful superordinate classification system within which we can better understand the unique contents of cultures.[41] Such analyses would, among other differences, recognize that socialization studies must extend well into adulthood, since moral reasoning development is known to continue, at least for some people, well beyond their twenties. Potentially, such development could occur at any time of life. Socialization researchers thus have additional theoretical support for studying lifelong learning.

Third, the analyses would closely examine the degree to which a society is a unified culture. In cases where cultural penetration is incomplete and where significant alternative cultures are present, the analyses would focus on the resulting intrasocietal conflicts. Analyses of such conflicts would be framed in terms of two separate dynamics:

1. The relative cognitive stages of the competing cultures would produce one set of dynamic forces. If the two stages differed from one another, the conflict would be marked by incomprehension of one culture by another, since the more complex structure cannot be expressed in terms of the less complex structure.[42] If the two cultures are at the same cognitive stage, their conflict will be unresolvable on strictly moral/cognitive grounds. Though the conflict may be ended by some sort of forceful subjugation of one culture by the other, the possibility will also always exist for a higher-stage resolution of the conflict. People who recognize the logical equivalence of the competing structures will feel a pressure, arising from their own intellectual integrity, to discover that resolution.

2. Another set of dynamic forces would arise from the requirements of establishing any way of relating as publicly common. Analyses here would focus on strategic and tactical advantages possessed by the members of the alternative cultures: control over the means of violence; economic power; immersion in traditional symbolism; and so on.

The analyses would look not just at a society's "extensive coherence"—the proportion of people adhering to a single culture—but also its "internal coherence"—the extent to which the cognitive structure of, say, economic relationships matches that of, say, governmental relationships. Kohlberg's studies of individual cognitive development show that an individual's moral development proceeds fairly uniformly across a wide range of moral issues; social scientists must examine whether the same is true of cultural ways of relating across the range of social relationships.

Social scientists also must study how subcultures relate to their cultures and to other subcultures. Which subcultures employ ways of relating differing in cognitive structure from the remainder of the culture? What role do such differences play in dissent and cultural change? Both cultural diffusion and revolution surely are affected by cognitive-structural considerations, and social scientists will have to look afresh at culture change theories.

The reward of such efforts is not just the theoretical virtue of using a well-defined concept of culture. An even greater reward comes in the rich hypotheses made possible by the formulation. Political development, for example, can be defined in terms of the cognitive structures of political cultures; this approach yields new hypotheses about developmental dynamics and stages of political society (Chilton, 1988b:Chapter 5). Even apart from such comprehensive theories, political scientists can study how politics varies across different cultures that have the same cognitive structure: i.e., what content variation is possible when structure is held constant? For example, are all Stage 2 cultures feudal in nature? Are Stage 2 feudal systems different from Stage 2 patron systems? If so, does this difference have political importance? Social scientists need a taxonomy of cultural possibilities in order to understand whether challenges to a culture will create a new cognitive structure or mere cultural shifts within the same cognitive structure. For example, in what way is the new Soviet political culture simply old autocratic wine in new Communist bottles, as theorists of Soviet political culture have asked?

Transposing the analytic matrix, social scientists can study how politics varies within a single cultural tradition when the structure changes. To what extent is there a "modernity of tradition," where traditional institutions bend to, but do not break against, new modes of thought? This hypothesis contradicts the just-cited "old wine in new bottles" hypothesis, and a rigorous cognitive-structural analysis could directly test these competing hypotheses.

In sum, the proposed reconceptualization of culture has implications throughout social science and particularly political science. If the political involves power and legitimacy, as Weber has it, then the concept of culture advanced here is quintessentially political: incorporating legitimacy in its study of how moral reasoning is structured; incorporating power in its study of how public commonness is established.[43]

Notes

1. "Political culture may provide us with a valuable conceptual tool by means of which we can bridge the 'micro–macro' gap in political theory. How does one make the transition from the study of the individual in his political context to the study of the political system as a whole? How does one relate individual interviews and responses, and case studies of individual actions, to the aggregate statistics and group behavior patterns which reflect the course of a system's total behavior? Political culture by revealing the patterns of orientations to political action helps us connect individual tendencies to system characteristics" (Almond and Powell, 1966:51–52).

2. Almond (1956:396) speaks evocatively of this constraint as an *embedding*. See also Almond and Powell's (1966:21–25) discussion of the relationship between structure and culture.

3. Almond (1956:397ff.) emphasizes the term's applicability across distinct political systems.

4. Most works on political culture discuss some theoretical issues. The following discussion relies primarily on Bunch (1971), Dittmer (1977), Kavanagh (1972), Lehman (1972), Pateman (1971), and Pye (1972).

5. Kim's 1964 review article presented the variety of conceptualizations that had appeared by then. See also the discussion in Sections III and IV of this chapter.

6. Some researchers retreat to raw empiricism: "These different definitions, however, need not preoccupy us, since most of the disputes are related less to what political culture is about than to the methodology to be employed when studying it" (Shafir, 1983:394).

7. "Such a definition is convenient for those interested in comparing and measuring the political cultures of different societies via the survey method; but it suffers from allowing one's methodological preference to define one's theoretical formulations" (Lehman, 1972:362). Contrast Shafir's comment in the previous note.

8. I do restrict my discussion to "social culture" (how people relate to one another) as opposed to "physical culture" (how people relate to their physical world).

9. "The terms which I shall use ... have emerged out of the Weber–Parsons tradition in social theory" (Almond, 1956:393). See also Almond (1956: *passim*), Almond and Verba (1963), Bunch (1971), Dittmer (1977), Kavanagh (1972), Lehman (1972), and Pateman (1971).

10. Dittmer (1977), Kavanagh (1972), Pye (1972), and Scheuch (1968).

11. The discussion offered here is sufficient justification of the criterion, but a further argument can be made that this criterion is crucial to solving the micro–macro problem. Conceptualizations that insist all actors equally determine the culture do not permit an analysis of emergent, unintended, or unrecognized effects of macro-level structures on individuals and culture. Specifically, such conceptualizations cannot even frame the macro–micro issues of false consciousness, nondecision-making, or structural power.

12. By social behavior I mean all action undertaken in coordination with other actors, whether or not those actors are present. Even private behavior—writing this piece, for example—contemplates an imagined audience, a "Generalized Other" (Hewitt, 1979:59–60).

13. John Miller (1984:42–46) argues that insistence on clear hypotheses and objective testability can inhibit fruitful interpretive analysis. Still, we should not make a virtue of a disagreeable necessity: *cet. par.*, clear, testable hypotheses must remain our goal.

14. The formulation of political culture by Almond and Verba (1963) differs in a small but theoretically crucial respect from that of Almond (1956). The earlier formulation

emphasized shared patterns of orientation, but the later formulation was based on a methodological individualism that subordinated mutual orientations to aggregations of isolation.

Additional studies in the *Civic Culture* tradition include Putnam (1976), Foster (1982), Szalay and Kelly (1982), and most contributors to Almond and Verba (1980). These authors examine different individual characteristics, but they all use population distributions to describe the political cultures they study.

15. "Our classification does not imply homogeneity or uniformity of political cultures" (Almond and Verba, 1963:20).

16. Elite studies (e.g., Putnam, 1976) attempt to meet the inequality criterion by aggregating the responses of a putative elite. As argued earlier, the conceptualization of political culture lying behind these methods fails to satisfy criteria 1, 2, and 9. Insofar as the elite studies are attempting to determine elite culture, they also fail to satisfy the inequality criterion: all elite actors are given equal weight, and no allowance is made for hegemonic control within the elite. Nor does a differential weighting scheme offer a solution, because the weights themselves can be assigned only ad hoc or—an infinite logical regression—on the basis of prior knowledge of the culture.

17. The role of political parties in the political system is a major emphasis of the work. Again, this is an unfortunate shift from Almond's (1956) original formulation.

18. Elazar's tradition is difficult to characterize, because Elazar studies political culture differently from his followers (e.g., Johnson, 1976, Hill, 1981, and Lowery and Sigelman, 1982), who simply employ culture as a three-valued, categorical, independent variable describing states or cities and who correlate it with political-structural or output variables. This form of research concentrates on political culture's correlates, not its conceptualization, and a reader of this literature may be pardoned for concluding that political culture is itself a political-structural concept. Elazar's followers use, but do not more clearly conceptualize, Elazar's original work, so it is to Elazar's work itself we must look for theoretical grounding.

19. Elazar's conceptualization need not suffer from these problems, in my opinion, but the absence of any clear formulation of his position, combined with his citation of questionable conceptualizations, lays him open to such objections.

20. See, for example, the Greenberg (1970) and Jaros, Hirsch, and Fleron (1968) studies of attitudes toward political leadership. (Cited in Jennings and Niemi, 1974:5n.)

21. There are actually several such traditions or schools of research. The idea that people exercise differential control over symbols pervades the Marxian tradition, from Marx onward. This idea is also found among the recent critics of pluralism (e.g., Stone, 1980), symbolic interactionists (e.g., Hewitt, 1979), and just plain students of symbols (e.g., Edelman, 1964, Elder and Cobb, 1983, and Nimmo and Combs, 1983).

22. Cuthbertson (1975:11) notes the importance of myths, one symbolic form: "Having myths is a shared characteristic of all societies. Indeed myth is the prerequisite of society." Dittmer (1977:565–583 passim) notes the interest of social anthropologists in symbols.

23. A way of relating is a standard for engaging in interaction: a method of defining situations, selecting alternatives, and acting. Weber's ideal-typical bureaucracy provides a concrete example of one "way of relating." A bureaucrat's action is interpreted in terms of its bureaucratic meaning: legal within the rules; not legal; or irrelevant to the rules—in which latter case it is outside the way of relating. Action within the rules can be judged as more or less rational, giving bureaucrats a way of selecting specific actions within a broad array of alternative courses permitted under the rules. Judgments of rationality even apply when choosing rules themselves, thus allowing bureaucrats to make and adapt their organizational framework to changing circumstances. This example shows that a way of relating is not any specific set of actions but is rather a way of understanding

and coordinating action. Ways of relating involve not simply isolated actions but rather many actual and potential actions integrated in a web of meaning, as Geertz (1973:3–30) argues. Thus the phrase "ways of relating" focuses simultaneously on the intended mutuality of behavior, whether or not the Other is present, and on the complete network of action alternatives.

24. I am indebted here to Prof. Edward Portis, whose objections led me to clarify this argument. The distinction between symbols and ways of relating closely resembles that made by Basil Bernstein (1966) and Mary Douglas (1982) between restricted codes (religion as ritual) and elaborated codes (religion as ethics). I am indebted to Aaron Wildavsky for bringing this tradition to my attention.

25. Brown (1977:1) recognizes this characteristic of culture when he includes "the *foci* of identification and loyalty" (my emphasis) and "political . . . expectations" in his conceptualization of political culture. Note that "public" does not mean "official." Widespread bribery may in certain countries be "public" (that is, adopted without discussion and with perfect understanding by all concerned in any transaction) even as it is "officially" condemned.

26. This is, of course, closely related to the position of "structural elitists" like Stone (1980).

27. Even the name, *symbolic interactionism,* connects symbols and ways of relating. See Hewitt (1979) for an excellent introduction.

28. Hence our ability to move easily back and forth between Dittmer's "symbol" conceptualization of political culture and the present "ways of relating" conceptualization.

29. The term "structure" has been applied to individual cognition, cultural ways of relating, and empirical patterns of behavior. The resulting terminological confusion is unfortunate but unavoidable. The term "structuralism" is sometimes applied to the approaches of the anthropologist Claude Levi-Strauss and the linguist Noam Chomsky. Piagetian structuralism differs significantly from those structuralisms because of Piaget's "functionalist" attention to explaining how structures originate and develop (Piaget, 1970:esp. Chapters 5 and 6).

30. The following argument is, in effect, a justification of the "postbehavioral" criterion.

31. Habermas (1983) discusses how the theoretical status of social science is affected by the unique necessity of social scientists studying action systems in what he calls the "performative attitude." He also discusses the role that justification in discourse plays in social action.

32. Flavell (1968), Selman (1971), Piaget (1977), Habermas (1979:esp.69–129), Higgins, Ruble, and Hartup (1983), and Overton (1983) discuss various aspects of the general connection among moral reasoning, role-taking, and social behavior. Berti, Bombi, and Lis (1982) and Berti, Bombi, and De Bene (1986) describe the Piagetian developmental acquisition of economic conceptions about means of production, owners, and profit. Habermas (1975, 1979) has been particularly concerned with the relationships among social behavior, moral reasoning, and the state's ability to legitimize its rule. See Piaget (1932), Kohlberg (1984a), and Colby et al. (1983) for general discussions of the moral development research tradition. See Kohlberg (1981) and Kohlberg, Levine, and Hewer (1984a) for a discussion of the claims presented here. Attacks on these claims can be found in Fishkin (1982), Gilligan (1982), Gibbs (1977), and other authors cited in Kohlberg, Levine, and Hewer (1984b). The latter work contains Kohlberg's replies to those attacks.

In view of the arguments surrounding Kohlberg's work, I will clarify its role in this argument. The present conceptualization only requires that *some* sequence of stages satisfy the five claims given in the text below. Critics like Gilligan (1982) and Gibbs (1977) attack only Kohlberg's particular sequence, conceding that some such sequence must exist. That is all this argument requires. (Some critics—Geertz, 1984, for example—deny the possibility of any such sequence.) I personally have only the most minor quarrels with the stage definitions. (See Chilton, 1988b:Chapter 3.)

33. Specific definitions of the stages are lengthy and are not required for the purposes of this essay. The interested reader should consult Kohlberg (1984), Colby and Kohlberg (1987), or *DPD* (Chilton, 1988b:Chapter 3). The six stages are termed Stage 1, Stage 2 ... Stage 6. Cognitive stages below Stage 1 differentiate morality so little from other concepts that they are not of much theoretical or (given their rarity in the adult population) practical interest, and Stage 6 does not occur with sufficient frequency to allow an empirical test of Kohlberg's philosophical argument for its developmental location or even its existence. There is a transitional period (possibly a stage) of extreme philosophical relativism between Stages 4 and 5: Stage 4 1/2. Colby and Kohlberg (1987) present Kohlberg's method of stage scoring, and Colby et al. (1983) present data on scoring reliability.

34. The stages of moral reasoning are most emphatically not evaluations of people's moral worth. A person employing Stage 1 reasoning is no less and no more worthy of having her claims to moral treatment respected than a person employing Stage 6 reasoning. Just as philosophers critique one another's positions as ambiguous and having unfortunate implications, without thereby condemning one another as evil people, so does the sequence of stages systematize and abstract the critiques in terms of reasoning structures, without thereby condemning the various reasoners (Kohlberg, 1981:esp. Parts One and Two).

35. Different societies have different mixtures of stages. Research suggests that moral reasoners in preliterate societies rarely or never develop beyond Stage 3. I reemphasize the previous footnote's caution: while we may evaluate moral reasoning as more or less adequate, we cannot judge the reasoners themselves as good or bad people, and thus even less can we extend evaluation to entire collections of reasoners. (See Chapter 8 below. See also Chilton [1988b: Chapter 5] for a description of the interactions among social structural change, cultural change, and individual development.)

36. Kohlberg, Levine, and Hewer (1984a) discuss the distinction between structure and content. Eberhardt (1984) illustrates the necessity of understanding a culture before interpreting its members' reasoning. Cross-cultural studies of reasoning obviously will have many methodological difficulties, but such difficulties alone do not constitute theoretical impossibilities.

37. See Colby and Kohlberg (1987). Other tests of moral reasoning make use of the facts that people at a given stage both prefer and can recapitulate arguments at that level. Preference forms the basis for Rest's (1973) test of moral judgment. Turiel (1966) and Selman (1971) explore the ability of people to recapitulate moral reasoning at different stages.

38. Even here structural analysis is anticipated by McClelland's (1976) and Aronoff's (1967, 1970) theme analyses. Radding's (1978, 1979) arguments are directly cognitive-structural.

39. Chilton (1984) discusses the practical consequences of such methodological alternatives.

40. Previous work in political culture has certainly shown what societies are important to study, for both their practical and theoretical interest: the United States, Great Britain, France, Italy, Mexico, Germany; the collectivist cultures of the Soviet Union and Eastern Europe; the non-Western cultures of China, Japan, Burma; the cultures of medieval Europe and England; the bureaucrats, political leaders, and activists in various polities; and so on. If we reconstruct our concept of political culture, we will need this reevaluation of our former analyses to see to what extent their results carry over beyond the aggregated individual to political culture itself.

41. It is interesting to note that many recent U.S. politics texts devote more space to processes of socialization into U.S. culture than to a description of its content. While the proposed conceptualization of political culture is already known to have strong implications for socialization (Hess and Torney, 1967), it also appears to be uniquely useful in helping analysts come to grips with cultural content.

42. Here I assume that the major difference is the stage difference. If the cultures' contents differ substantially, the incomprehension would undoubtedly be mutual.

43. Cognitive development and the establishment of public commonness are the two central dynamics of political development. See *DPD* (Chilton, 1988b:Chapter 5).

7

Culture Is the
Locus of Development

If the concept of development exists, as we assume, then it must refer to a change in some *thing* and thus its definition must take the following form: "X is said to undergo political development when X changes from state PD1 to state PD2."[1] Even if we don't know exactly what PD1 and PD2 are, or how to characterize them, we can still ask what "thing" develops during development. X is said to be the *locus* of development. What is the "X" in such a definition?

I. Three Potential Systems
Within Which To Locate Development

Both Talcott Parsons (Parsons and Shils, 1951) and Jüergen Habermas (1979a) divide the universe of social-scientific concepts into three parts. In Parsons's theory, concepts describe events within three "systems": the "personality" or "individual" system, the "cultural" system, and the "social" system. The individual system includes all concepts that refer to purely intrapsychic events—concepts that can meaningfully characterize a person considered in isolation. Such concepts as "moral reasoning stage" (Kohlberg, 1981, 1984), "subject orientation" (Almond and Verba, 1963) and "need for Achievement" (McClelland, 1976) all refer to intrapsychic events.

Another way of characterizing concepts in the individual system is to use Habermas's (1979a) idea of a "validity claim": Parsons's individual system is composed of concepts that only raise the Habermasian validity claim of "truthfulness." Possession of a need for Achievement, for example, is established only by a person's being truthful about her own experience; issues of intersubjective agreement or of objective truth are irrelevant. A person may have no objective reason to have a need for Achievement, or may find its exercise hampered by her intersubjective understandings with others, but one cannot deny that ultimately her truthful assertion is all that is required to establish the existence of such a need. The validity claim here is one of subjective validity.

Note, however, that the individual system's reference to "intrapsychic events" does not require that the actor be completely isolated; it means, rather, that possession of this characteristic does not depend on any particular action of others. For example, "moral reasoning stage" would be a meaningless concept in a universe having only one inhabitant, but to hold a given set of moral principles does not depend on others' actions or beliefs. The individual system also includes aggregates or averages of such intrapsychic concepts when the aggregate is not held to have any emergent properties. Thus the "average level of need for Achievement" of a collectivity would be a concept still within the individual system.

The cultural system, on the other hand, refers to people's intersubjective understandings—their mutual orientations to one another. The cultural system is thus composed of relationships. For example, to be in the cultural-system relationship of friendship requires someone else's participation: i.e., one's friend. To feel friendly toward someone, on the other hand, does not require the other's cooperation; such a feeling would be part of the individual system.

Cultural-system concepts raise only the validity claim of "rightness" (Habermas, 1979a). To determine the existence of a relationship of friendship demands that both parties agree that friendly behavior is right within the context of their mutual orientation. The validity claim here is one of intersubjective agreement.

Finally, the social system refers to objective patterns of interaction, such as those revealed in sociometric matrices of contacts or other interaction measures employed in social psychology.[2] The presence of a pecking order in chickens, for example, is an objectively measurable phenomenon that does not depend for its verification on the subjective (individual-system) beliefs of the various chickens or on knowledge of the intersubjective (cultural-system) understandings they have established. The recognition of such interaction patterns only raises what Habermas (1979a) terms the validity claim of "truth": does the pattern objectively exist?

We distinguish these three systems in order to ask what it is that changes in political development: something in the individual system, something in the cultural system, or something in the social system? In other words, is development at root a matter of changes in individuals (or aggregate changes in individuals), in the way people relate to one another, or in the objective patterns of their interactions?

The choice is not obvious. Because the three systems are closely tied to one another, the exact locus of development is difficult to determine. Aggregations of individual characteristics are bound to affect cultural understanding, if only by determining outer limits on the possibilities. Cultural understandings are bound to affect individuals through well-known mechanisms of socialization and peer pressure. Common, cultural understandings will also inevitably create regular patterns of interaction as cultural institutions induce regularities of behavior. Even regularities of behavior that initially arise from accident or impersonal forces can give rise to cultural understandings as the participants recognize, come to expect, and finally name these patterns.[3] Particularly in stable societies, where the three systems have the opportunity to accommodate themselves to one another, distinguishing among the three systems may be both difficult and apparently unimportant. It is not surprising, therefore, that different theorists have located political development in different systems.

As we shall see, however, a concept of development would be located more plausibly in one of these systems than the others. But to determine which, we shall have to concentrate on societies in which the three systems are not in equilibrium. In other words, locating political development in one of the three systems strongly depends on recognizing that development involves *dis*equilibrium, and asking which of the three systems most suits our understanding of development in a situation of change.

II.   Individual-System Definitions and Their Problems

There have been many individual-system definitions of political development. The best-known of these, that implied in *The Civic Culture,* defines political development in terms of a particular "distribution of patterns of orientation" (Almond and Verba, 1963:13). Since such patterns are "distributed," they evidently must not depend on other citizens also holding them. They are thus part of the individual system, and their aggregation across citizens is also part of the individual system; in this formulation, political development depends by definition only on the mixture of individuals involved.[4] McClelland (1976) might be read to give a similar (individual-level) definition of development: average level of need for Achievement.[5]

The difficulty with such definitions is that people can change their minds faster than they can their institutional practices. A massive shift in the sentiments of a population might well lead to changes in their political institutions, but such institutional responses ordinarily take time. Would we consider developed a society in which the population widely and genuinely believed in freedom of speech but whose police systematically harassed and arrested all dissidents? Would we consider developed a society in which the population generally had a high need for Achievement, but all were constrained to a bare living as tenant farmers? When we think of development, we think of institutional arrangements that may depend on but nevertheless pass beyond individual desires, even in their aggregate.

Conversely, political institutions can change without much shift in population sentiment at all: the Weimar Republic of 1932 and the Third Reich of 1933 both governed virtually the same population. If we define development in terms of individual characteristics alone, we would be forced to regard the two states as equally developed.

These problems arise no matter what individual characteristic we select: "patterns of orientation," psychological needs, moral reasoning levels, etc. Such characteristics may well affect development or arise from it, but the basic point remains that political development itself seems to pass beyond individual characteristics, even aggregated characteristics.

III.   Social System Definitions and Their Problems

It is possible to define political development in terms of social-system patterns of interaction. One might define it by the absence of interactions characterized by force, or by density of linkages, or by the frequency of "power cycles."[6] In fact, Moreno (1934) intended his early work on sociometric analysis as a means of studying which groups would survive and which would not. Such social-system definitions of development are still virtually unknown in the literature, perhaps due to the difficulty of observing and analyzing interaction patterns in a national society,[7] but they remain a theoretical possibility.

Whether such definitions are theoretically adequate is another question, however. Such definitions lack any sense of moral meaning. An objective pattern of interaction cannot be evaluated (i.e., as representing "development" or its reverse) apart from the meanings attached to it by its participants. One can infer such meanings, but then one is evaluating not the social-system phenomenon—the objective pattern—but instead an (inferred) cultural-system or individual-system phenomenon. Is it development, for example, when the density of linkages increases? One can only say, "It depends." If the increase arises from greater social cohesiveness, then presumably it would be developmental. If the increase arises from overpopulation in a fixed living space, then presumably it is not. The point is that objective phenomena do not provide one with the information one seeks to make judgments of development. Objective phenomena can reflect such information, of course; this is what makes them useful to study. But if we are to determine the actual *locus* of development, we must look to development itself, not phenomena that merely reflect it.

Indeed, it is possible to produce patterns of interaction without any cultural or individual meaning attached to them at all. Consider a set of people divided into several subsets, each of which has no contacts with other subsets. Suppose further this objective pattern changed so that there were no longer distinct subsets. Such a change might appear developmental (in some quasi-Kantian sense that the basis of interaction had become more universal), but it might not be. It might be that the original subsets were desert dwellers drinking at different oases, all but one of which then dried up. The subsets need not be groups in any social sense, and their interactions no more than accidental contacts when visiting the oasis. In short, objective patterns tell us nothing about the moral meanings we infer to assess development: our inferences may be totally incorrect, and the necessity we feel to make them reveals that we locate development in other systems.

IV.   Cultural-System Definitions and Their Problems

Could development be located in the cultural system? In other words, could it be thought of as involving at least a change in people's intersubjective understandings with one another?[8] This possibility has at least a face validity, in that it is not subject to the problems of definitions located in the other systems. (1) Unlike objective patterns of interaction, intersubjective understandings have normative valence: they are evaluable against ethical standards. (2) A problem with locating development in objective patterns of interaction is that we must infer what produces the pattern; such inferences seem to be to intersubjective understandings, which could certainly produce the objective patterns. (3) One of the problems with using the individual system was that people could change individually without such change necessarily producing institutional change. Since institutions are based on intersubjective understandings, locating development in the cultural system surmounts that objection. (4) Finally, intersubjective understandings can change even while the individuals retain the same basic orientations.[9]

Locating development in the cultural system is not without its problems, however. In particular, even though we think of societies developing, intersubjective understandings may not embrace the whole society. As Almond and Verba (1963) showed, people have substantially different understandings of how they are to relate to one another politically: some relate as mutual participants in a law-making process; some relate as fellow citizens maintaining but merely subject to a preexisting legal order; and some relate in a fashion characterized by inattention to political and legal considerations. Does this diversity argue for a return to Almond and Verba's individual-system locus of development, where development is the aggregate of these different orientations?

I hold that it does not—that we can conceive of development more naturally as a property of cultures than of societies. Societies tend to be defined "top-down"—that is, to be defined by criteria apart from any intersubjective understandings they may contain. U.S. society, for example, is defined in terms of a geographical boundary, not in terms of anything necessarily shared among its inhabitants. Since societies are inevitably diverse, analysts are put in the position of trying to determine the resulting mixture of (individual, because no longer shared) orientations. If, on the other hand, we define culture "from the bottom up," as discussed in Chapter 6, then we can speak of development as occurring when that understanding changes in certain specific ways. Top-down definitions create endless problems: determining where one mixture shades into another; identifying which orientation is politically dominant; and so on. Bottom-up definitions, on the other hand, allow analysts to characterize clearly the understanding and its developmental status. The developmental dynamics of societies as a whole can then be studied in terms of the political interactions of these disparate cultures.

V. Conclusion

If development is an individual-system phenomenon, then the problems of the Third World are merely psychological in nature, not political: development workers must be psychiatrists at best and advertising specialists at worst, all in an effort to get every developing nation's residents in the right frame of mind. If development is a social-system phenomenon, then the problems of development are merely those of putting the world's citizens through the right rituals. Development workers can paint colored lines on floors and can put signs on walls to indicate where people should walk, where they should interact, what they should do. Perhaps a "How To Be Developed" manual could be mass-produced and distributed.

But of course all this is silly. If development indeed exists as a concept, it must be located in the cultural system, and the task of development workers must therefore be the quite difficult one of facilitating the establishment of certain intersubjective understandings despite existing, quite different understandings. Such a task demands not just that people change their own mind about how to orient to one another but also that they become aware that others will reciprocate this new orientation. The complexity of this process explains, it seems to me, why fostering development has traditionally been so difficult.

The question still remains, however, what *is* development? This chapter argues that if such a concept exists, then it must be located in the cultural system, but the argument does not say how to identify which cultural changes are developmental and which not. That task raises not only the question of identifying development but also the difficult question of how one is to justify a given change as "up." That problem, of "normative grounding," is addressed in *DPD*, Chilton (1988a), and Rosenberg, Ward, and Chilton (1988).

Notes

1. PD1 and PD2 could be described directly or could be specified only in terms of salient characteristics by which we may know they have appeared.

2. For example, communication studies focus on "who says what to whom, and with what effect." The interpretations of the "what" and "with what effect" lie within the individual and cultural systems, but the bare fact of person X saying something to person Y and the regularities of such communication (frequency, reciprocity, etc.) lie within the social system.

3. For example, accidentally coinciding course schedules may bring a group of professors together for lunch, but the group's members can bond to create a new cultural understanding that they are a "lunch group."

4. In fact, Almond and Verba conclude that a mixture in the population of "subject" and "participant" orientations is best.

5. McClelland never specifically defines development but rather argues that need for Achievement is a cause of economic growth (per capita GNP).

6. Frey (1963:301n). Power cycles are the opposite of a pecking order. In a pecking order, X_1 exerts power over X_2, X_2 over X_3, and so on. In a power cycle, X_1 exerts power over X_2, X_2 over X_3, etc., and finally X_n over X_1. Democracy could be defined in terms of the presence of such cycles.

7. Having employed such an analysis, Chilton (1977:367ff.) concludes that the observational and computational requirements are extreme, even for relatively small groups (N = 80, 103, and 160).

8. Before his work with Verba led him to change his definition to a more individual-system one, Almond (1956:396) defined political culture in terms of such intersubjective understandings: the "particular pattern of orientations to political action."

9. For example, consider the shift in intersubjective understanding that two people would experience when, terrified by meeting each other in a dark alley, they suddenly discover by the light of a passing car the face of an old friend.

8

The "Ways of Relating" Perspective

I. Our Relations With Others

In this and the next chapter I want to discuss the general rationale behind my approach to political development. I don't mean the narrow logic of my argument, which stands or falls by the arguments advanced either in the previous chapters of this work or in *DPD*. I mean instead some general considerations that led me to look for this sort of conception. Because those considerations first coalesced for me in the phrase "ways of relating," this chapter discusses the phrase's connotations and clarifies some of the complexities of its usage.

As I argued in Chapter 6, people relate to one another in ways that have an overall coherence, at least insofar as the individuals share the same culture. The phrase "ways of relating" is intended to convey this image of coherence among different relations. Political, economic, and social institutions, whether formal or informal, simply embody possible ways of dealing with each other. Our support of, opposition to, acquiescence in, or creation of such institutions represents how we choose to relate to others. Moral philosophies, principles of justice, care, responsibility, or obligation—all these simply describe ways of relating to people.

But the connotations of the phrase extend a little beyond mere coherence: I also intend the phrase to imply that we must look at our relationships with all others. We all have a moral relationship with every other human being on the planet, whatever character that relationship might take.[1] Even the denial of relationship is, in this view, only one possible way that people relate to one another. For example, to deny a relationship with someone on the grounds that they are not a fellow citizen is simply to affirm that our relationships with people will differ according to their citizenship.

There is both less here than meets the eye, and more. On the one hand, I am not making a sentimental argument that we owe the same things to all people (love, responsibility, care, etc.). It seems clear that we are concerned for those close to us in a way that we cannot be for those far away. To say that I have relationships with all humans is more an analytical, almost tautological, statement than a characterization of those relationships.

But on the other hand, this framework does have some bite, in two ways. First, the perspective pointedly insists that in choosing the character of our

95

relationships, we recognize the implications of these ways of relating for everyone, not just for those admitted to our moral universe. Our relationships are often used to divide those to whom we must explain our actions from those to whom no such explanations are deemed necessary. For example, many people hold themselves answerable to their fellow citizens but cannot conceive of having obligations independent of those defined by law. Their moral discourse would revolve around the legal-illegal distinction, to which they hold themselves and their fellow citizens equally bound. But since this distinction breaks down when dealing with citizens of other countries, moral discourse becomes impossible. So the first consequence of this perspective is to require us, when justifying how we will relate to others, to discuss what character we want any particular relationship to have, not whether the relationship exists in the first place.

The second consequence of this perspective is to require that we face the Other mutually and reciprocally. This requirement applies even to those we know poorly, although obviously more time would be required to work through many miscommunications. Phrasing this point in the negative, the perspective means that our justifications to one another cannot be simply a Hobbesian stand-off of egoisms; as Gaus (1990) argues, such an impoverished view of our obligations to one another would require us to give up almost everything of what we consider human.

The recognition of all relationships provides a check on our moral categories. When supporting an institution, or choosing a set of moral principles, or making a moral decision, we have to be able to face in honor and mutual respect every other person, if only in our imagination, and affirm as our relationship what this institution, principle, or decision represents. We cannot avoid the issue by claiming that the Other is somehow not part of our moral universe.

This is, I believe, a key aspect of John Rawls's (1971) theory. Choosing among principles of justice behind the "veil of ignorance" in the "original position," people do not know their interests, talents, or social position, and so are forced to consider their relationship with all other people. Whether Rawls's two principles would indeed be chosen under these conditions is not my concern here; what I wish to point out is that the conditions of the original position implicitly recognize relations among all people.[2]

I should note that even though relationships "flatten out" as we deal with people increasingly distant from us (as I argue later), we still owe something— respect, reciprocity, justice—to everybody. Our debt may of necessity be impersonal, but it cannot be inhumane.

II.   Feminist Critcisms of Abstracted Relations

Mentioning Rawls leads me to criticisms by feminist scholars (e.g., Gilligan, 1982; Benhabib, 1986; Fraser, 1986) of general, abstract notions of our interrelations represented by the work of Rawls (1971), Lawrence Kohlberg (1981,

1984), and Jüergen Habermas (1979), hereafter referred to as "Rawls (etc.)" Feminists make essentially two points in attacking general theories of social justice. First, they argue that such general theories, spoken in the (male) voice of rights and duties, fail to address concerns of care and responsibility that are spoken in the different (female) voice.[3] They argue that we need to meet people in their particularity, where issues of care and responsibility are more important than those of abstract rights and justice. Second, they argue that attention to the general as opposed to the particular effectively silences people outside the power structure (e.g., women, minorities, etc.). In their view, the Rawlsian "original position," whatever its theoretical merits, becomes *in practice* the forum of white, upper-class males. Even if those villains are willing to assume a "veil of ignorance," abjuring any knowledge of their estates, the dominance of white, upper-class, male understandings of the world would remain.[4]

The perspective of this chapter's first section would seem subject to such attacks.[5] The very language used there (e.g., that we face people "if only in the imagination") contemplates what Benhabib (1986) terms the "generalized" as opposed to the "concrete" other.

But these objections are unpersuasive. First, the charge that Rawls (etc.) ignores particularity ignores the possibility of a reasonable division of moral labor. The web of our relationships with people "thickens" as they become nearer to us, not because they are more deserving of fundamental ethical respect but rather because our calculations can be more attentive to their particular situation. There is nothing *inherently* wrong with adopting as a policy that everyone devote more care and take more responsibility for those close to them than for those more distant.[6]

The division of moral labor means that our concern "flattens out" as we attend to people increasingly distant from us. This flattening reflects not a lessening of concern but rather the decreasing particularity of that concern—a shift away from responsibility and towards justice. As Fraser (1986) points out, theories rooted in the concrete other are limited to the small frame and thus are not helpful in considering how we are to relate even to our fellow citizens, much less to all people. Theories of justice concern what we owe to all people, while theories of care and responsibility "overlay" them.[7] This overlay is most prominent in our dealings with people close to us, so that we are only rarely concerned with the broader dictates of justice. As we turn our attention to people more distant from us, however, our sense of *particular* care and responsibility decreases, so that our concerns become increasingly dictated by the underlying configuration of our theory of justice, based on a sense of generalized, even impersonal, care. Although I don't know any starving Sudanese, I do know that care includes eating. The sense of universal relationship provides reason for acting, even if the action necessarily cannot be individualized.

The second feminist objection, of bias in practice, needs to be taken seriously, inasmuch as public discourse in U.S. society (and undoubtedly all societies) is not that of free and equal citizens. But this objection has a peculiar status. It is not a theoretical objection, claiming that the approach of Rawls (etc.) to justice is inherently oppressive. Instead, the objection is practical, demanding that Rawls (etc.) provide some assurance that their perspective can be carried out in practice. Rawls (etc.) cannot simply hypothesize that the discourse in the original position is that of free and equal citizens, and then blandly ignore the practical difficulties of conducting such discourse. Thus this second feminist objection can only be met by a practical political platform committed to an ongoing critical stance toward existing forms of domination.

Rawls and his fellow generalists are at least cognizant of these practical concerns. For example, Rawls (1971) clearly does not want to rest with an idealized original position, since he emphasizes that one of the problems with utilitarianism, and thus one reason to prefer his theory, is that utilitarianism does not take seriously the difference among persons. The ideally sympathetic individual contemplated by utilitarians cannot substitute, in Rawls's view, for the concrete confrontation of different understandings. The truth of Rawls's assessment (that utilitarianism does not respect the difference among persons) is not the issue here. The point I am making is that Rawls sees his own theory as taking into account concrete differences among real people.

But awareness of the need for an emancipatory political practice is not the same as that practice, so we still face the objection that general theories provide no real mechanism for giving voice to the silent. The feminist objections point social theory towards practical concerns.[8] Feminists have established at least a prima facie case that theoretical discourse can become an unwitting agent of oppression. Social theory cannot overcome their objections simply by further theorizing; the intermingling of practical consequences with theoretical discourse requires a new, praxis-based social theory. Sooner rather than later, theoretical approaches must be disciplined by the demands of concrete social practice.[9]

Notes

1. Like Rawls (1985), I will not engage in an unresolvable, metaphysical debate over whether "relationships to all other humans" is a statement of some metaphysical reality, instead of merely a way of looking at moral issues. My claim is that the "ways of relating" perspective is useful, not that it is metaphysically or existentially "true." However, *contra* Rawls, this perspective *can* be extended to our relationships even to people who apparently have no sense of justice, and perhaps beyond: to animals and to all living things.

2. In later work, Rawls (1985) argues that his perspective does not imply any metaphysical claims about the nature of justice. He might argue, likewise, that he intends no such claims about any inherent relationship or lack thereof among human beings. But even given Rawls's limitation of his argument, some flavor of inherent interrelationship persists. First, the original position clearly incorporates relationships among all people within the liberal democratic societies Rawls says the "justice as fairness" perspective pertains to. Second, as Raz (1990) argues, Rawls's presentation of "a theory of *justice*, rather than a theory of social stability" (Raz, 1990:14) entails some claims about the nature of justice, one of these being that justice is characterized by consensus. Our

sharing common moral ground sufficient to achieve such a consensus in reflective equilibrium is a practical issue varying from situation to situation. Such sharing is not something to be built into the definition of justice itself.

3. This dichotomy between the male and female voice is of course not absolute; men can and do use the language of care and responsibility, and women can and do use the language of rights and duties (Ford and Lowery, 1986). The reference here to male and female voice is to tendency or preference, not a statement of some inherent, absolute division.

4. In Fraser's elegant description of this domination:

> By socio-cultural means of interpretation and communication I mean things like: the officially recognized vocabularies in which one can press claims; the idioms available for interpreting and communicating one's needs; the established narrative conventions available for constructing the individual and collective histories which are constitutive of social identity; the paradigms of argumentation accepted as authoritative in adjudicating conflicting claims; the ways in which various discourses constitute their respective subject matters as specific sorts of objects; the repertory of available rhetorical devices; the bodily and gestural dimensions of speech which are associated in a given society with authority and conviction. Suppose it were the case that by and large such socio-cultural means of interpretation and communication expressed the point of view of dominant groups in society (1986:425).

5. *DPD* relied to some extent on Kohlberg's work, and so weaknesses of Kohlberg's theory are implicitly weaknesses in *DPD*'s definition of political development. I am not dismissing Gilligan's (1982) objections to Kohlberg's (1981, 1984) work, merely its applicability to my concerns. Gilligan points out that Kohlberg's theory and scoring system pertain to the language of justice and abstract rights, not to the language of care and responsibility. Kohlberg (1984:Appendix A) in effect accepts this criticism by referring to "justice reasoning" instead of the previous "moral reasoning." As argued in *DPD* (Chilton, 1988b:63n.3), this concession does not alter *DPD*'s conception of political development. *DPD* bases its conception of political development on the development of structures of moral reasoning, not on Kohlberg's specific theory. Gilligan does not deny that some universal sequence of structural stages exists; she only denies that Kohlberg's particular stages embrace the universe of moral discourse.

6. Such a policy, like any other way of relating, has to be justified to everyone, but it certainly has a prima facie reasonableness, since we are more able to assume responsibilities and to adopt an attitude of care for those we know well than for those we do not. The pinch comes, of course, when we face those who are left worst off by this policy: the homeless; the elderly; the insane; the orphans—all those whose social connections have disappeared or worn away, so that the division of moral labor leaves them without support. Here it seems to me that a Rawlsian perspective is a natural one: will our caring less for those close to us advantage those more distant? To some extent it will, of course; the concern and responsibility foregone for those close to us can to some degree be converted to care for those more distant, through such institutions as shelters, orphanages, county nursing homes, residential treatment centers, and so on. However unsatisfactory these are, they certainly reflect concern for those whose social moorings have been cut. But it is an empirical question, and thus beyond the scope of this book, whether less attention to those close to us will benefit those more distant. At some point, failure to care for those close to us makes us unable to care for anyone at all, both because our own needs for companionship and intimate relations are not met and because we will have no concrete way to learn what relationship means.

7. Recall that Rawls's intention is to develop a theory of social justice applied to the basic structure, not to present a comprehensive theory of individual morality (Rawls, 1971:Section 2).

8. My understanding of the theoretical consequences of feminists' practical concerns has been enriched by Vaillancourt's (1986) description of Marxian theoretical approaches, even though Vaillancourt herself would probably not agree with the praxis-based approach advanced here.

9. This discipline is intellectual, not political. We must not *subordinate* theoretical discourse to political concerns. Theory and practice retain equal dignity, standing in dialectical opposition to each other.

9

The Political Practice
of Genetic Epistemology

Both *DPD* and this book rely heavily on an extension of Lawrence Kohlberg's micro-level, genetic-epistemological theory of the development of moral reasoning (Colby and Kohlberg, 1987; Kohlberg, 1981, 1984) to the macro level of social aggregates, producing a definition of political development and a theoretical framework for studying it. This extension is accordingly subject to two sets of criticisms and misunderstandings: those attacking Kohlberg's work itself and hence the validity of any theory based on it, and those attacking the extension of Kohlberg's micro findings to the macro level. The first purpose of this chapter is to review and rebut these objections.

However, as noted in the previous chapter, more than a simple rebuttal is necessary. The objections arise in part because the works in question imply, but fail to describe clearly, a society structured in accordance with genetic-epistemological principles. Since theoretical perspectives can easily front for concrete oppressions, people are naturally reluctant to adopt a perspective without seeing something of its practical consequences. Accordingly, this chapter presses beyond theoretical issues to statements about the political practice implied by the genetic-epistemological perspective.

The description of this political practice will be tentative and incomplete. Definite descriptions of social forms depend on the existence of those forms, and we have as yet little experience with them. The extension of the genetic-epistemological perspective to the real world must therefore be seen as "work in progress," and the statements made in this chapter as my best guess.

The chapter is organized in three sections. The first describes the genetic-epistemological perspective and its differences from other structuralist perspectives. The second section states the most common objections to genetic epistemology and its extension to political development, and it replies to them. The third section turns directly to the political practice implied by the genetic-epistemological perspective—in particular, the nature of politics within a society and the nature of development policy.

I.   Genetic Epistemology

Genetic epistemology[1] arises from the following observations:

1. Knowledge is not a direct apprehension or representation of the environment but is instead constituted in the interrelationship of physical actions or operations within an organized whole. This "structural" view of knowledge distinguishes genetic epistemology from the alternative epistemologies underlying stimulus–response theory, social learning theory, and the accumulation model (Hess and Torney, 1967). Such alternatives view knowledge as a set of associations between arbitrary elements, having no necessary logical structure. In these theories, "truth" is learned in the same manner as "falsehood"—assuming that such terms could even be given meaning within those theories. Genetic epistemology recognizes the abstract logical organization of knowledge.[2]

2. Structural forms of knowledge develop from the active construction of the world that arises during interaction with it; such knowledge does not develop from biological maturation (that is, such knowledge is not "wired in") or from associative learning (associative learning exists, of course, but it does not produce the logical structures we are speaking of). The world with which one interacts can be physical, social, or aesthetic. Interaction with the physical world produces a sequence of structures of physical-logical thought—structures that become increasingly stable in the face of shifts of perspective (Piaget).[3] Interaction with the social world produces a sequence of structures of moral judgment—structures that become increasingly stable in the face of shifts in one's position in the social situation (Kohlberg).[4] Interaction with the aesthetic world produces a sequence of structures of aesthetic judgment that become increasingly stable in the face of differences between different people's aesthetic experiences (Parsons).

This *constructivist, interactionist* position is characteristic of genetic-epistemological theories, and distinguishes them both from nonstructuralist theories and from other structuralist theories.[5] Only in genetic epistemology are the structures constructed by the actor (as opposed to existing immanently) and yet constructed not by the actor alone but rather as the actor interacts with the environment.

3. These philosophical and theoretical foundations of genetic epistemology are reinforced by a series of empirical findings listed earlier in Chapter 5.[6]

4. The structures constructed by each (inter-) actor develop in response to conflicts among alternative perspectives by successively differentiating to reestablish mutual coordination with one another. That is, structures develop when an actor discovers that the current structure yields different conclusions when applied to different perspectives; new structures arise as the actor develops a more refined or comprehensive logical structure so that the separate, formerly conflicting perspectives are recoordinated with one another.

Consider the following example from the physical world. Children often believe that the reason they see the moon in the same position relative to themselves, even when they move around, is that the moon is following them.

They discover the difficulties with this theory when they learn that their friends believe the moon follows them around, too. They are able to resolve this dilemma by differentiating their perspectives from others' and by coordinating these perspectives through an image of a Euclidean world.

Structural development is not inevitable, since it depends on the recognition that perspectives can conflict. This recognition may not occur, and may even be denied through psychological or sociological mechanisms. But development is always possible—for any person, at any stage, whenever she perceives such relativity (Flavell, 1963; Kohlberg, 1981, 1984a).

These processes also occur in the construction of moral and aesthetic knowledge, where one's moral or aesthetic perspective is repeatedly challenged by conflicting perspectives—others' perspectives, or one's own perspective at another time.

In each of the three domains of discourse, the resulting observable, sequential construction of cognitive structures yields a sequence of philosophically more adequate positions. As Kohlberg expresses it for the domain of moral reasoning:

> The scientific theory as to why people factually *do* move upward from stage to stage, and why they factually *do* prefer a higher stage to a lower, is broadly the same as a moral theory as to why people *should* prefer a higher stage to a lower. . . . [Although] psychological theory and normative ethical theory are not reducible to each other, the two enterprises are isomorphic or *parallel* (Kohlberg, 1981:179–180).

Thus there is a simultaneous, mutually disciplining construction of both the hypothesized cognitive structures of morality and our understanding of the nature of morality itself.[7]

5. Genetic epistemology speaks of individual development, but its findings can be applied to macro social structures as well.[8] The application must be cognizant of emergent properties of social aggregates, but it nevertheless permits a definition of political development (and a theoretical framework for studying it) that flows from the genetic-epistemological perspective (*DPD*; Rosenberg, Ward, and Chilton, 1988). Briefly, the individual-level perspective of genetic epistemology is translated to the macro-level perspective of political development by noting that cultures are defined by the particular ways of relating that are employed in social interaction; that ways of relating constitute moral reasoning; and that the moral reasoning employed by a specific culture can be stage-scored (Chapter 6 of this book). The structural ambiguities Kohlberg identifies in each stage carry over to social conflicts, providing one mechanism for developmental dynamics. However, development can also be affected by hegemonic control over what ways of relating are invented; if invented, which become prominent; and, if prominent, which are chosen for use. The process of development then arises from the interaction of these two

dynamic forces of structural ambiguity and hegemonic power (*DPD*, Chapter 5).

II.   Criticisms, Misinterpretations, and Replies

A.   *Criticisms and Misinterpretations*

Most philosophical criticisms of genetic epistemology (and its application to entire cultures) arise from critics' concerns about cultural relativism, since genetic epistemology explicitly judges reasoning structures as more or less adequate. Specific criticisms are as follows:[9]

1. Regardless of its empirical claims, the origin of genetic epistemology in the rationalist, male, Western, liberal tradition puts its normative claims out of court. This objection applies to both Kohlberg's theory of moral reasoning development and, before that, Piaget's theory of both logical and moral development.

2. That this origin of genetic epistemology dictates its results can be seen in several areas: in the almost complete absence of "high-stage" thinking among certain cultures (especially nonliterate cultures); in the relative absence of high-stage thinking among women; and in the scoring system's inability to recognize moral orientations frequently adopted by women. The highly skewed nature of the empirical results is held to falsify the perspective.

3. By arguing for the superiority of one form of reasoning over another, genetic epistemology is held to lack respect for the values of other cultures. It is no more than a scientistic justification for continued Western, capitalist, imperialist, and/or patriarchal oppression.

4. Kohlberg himself apparently denies any possible extension of his work to macro political structure:

> A related confusion of the relativist is the notion that the function of moral principles is to judge cultures or societies as wholes, and, because one cannot legitimately make absolute moral evaluations of one culture as worth more or less than another, there are no nonrelative moral principles. Moral principles, however, prescribe universal human obligations; *they are not scales for evaluating collective entities* (Kohlberg, 1981:111; emphasis supplied).

> We do not believe that the comparison of one culture to another in terms of moral development is a theoretically useful strategy for the growth of scientific knowledge.... Comparisons [of mean moral scores between cultures] have no scientific justification or value, since they would imply that it makes sense to speak of one culture having more moral worth than another. It is difficult to understand what a valid concept of "comparative moral worth of culture" might be, but in any case, such a concept could not be established on the basis of comparison of means on our moral judgment assessment scale. There is no direct way in which group averages can be translated into statements of the relative moral worth of groups.

Like most anthropologists, we would agree that cultures should be treated evaluatively as unique configurations of norms and institutions which help social organizations to adapt to local conditions as well as to universal normative problems. In this sense anthropological cultural relativism is compatible with our philosophic assumption of the universal validity of moral principles. . . . We do not understand how a "moral ranking" of cultures could either be done or be scientifically useful (Kohlberg, 1984:330–331).

B. *Replies*

The following replies are indexed to the objections listed above. The first three replies are based on Kohlberg, Levine, and Hewer (1984b); the second also owes much to Fraser (1986).

1. Arguments against a theory on the basis of its origin have no philosophical weight. Origins can make one suspicious of a theory, but to prove or disprove its assertions requires direct analysis. Philosophical or empirical claims made by a theory can only be challenged by philosophical counterargument or empirical disproof.

2. Moral development occurs most in those populations most exposed to wide-scale moral conflicts. Nonliterate societies tend to be small societies, where conflicts arise in the context of dyadic, face-to-face relations. Sex differences in moral reasoning levels appear in cultures where one sex is more restricted than the other. Studies controlling for education and occupational status reveal no sex differences in moral stage. (See Kohlberg, Levine, and Hewer, 1984b:345–348, citing Walker, 1982.)

However, it may be true, as Gilligan (1982), Benhabib (1986), Fraser (1986), and others have argued, that Kohlberg's scoring system does not recognize certain forms of moral discourse. It is certainly a theoretical possibility for any such cognitive development scoring system. Kohlberg (1984) himself grants the limitation of his own work by speaking of "justice reasoning" instead of "moral reasoning."

The problems of Kohlberg's specific scoring system are not relevant to the claims made in the present work, however. The heart of the genetic-epistemological perspective is the requirement for moral claims to be discursively justified. As Habermas (1983) points out, the abstract grounds explaining the normative power of any sequence of moral reasoning stages can only be determined retrospectively; such justification is always subject to new understandings. Because empirical studies of moral development must start from a philosophical position in regard to the nature of morality, they cannot be used to establish normative value, but they can be used to discipline such positions. Properly conceived criteria of moral judgment should produce empirical findings of invariant structural development. This interaction between philosophical argument and empirical discovery makes any specific view of morality subject to challenge on both philosophical and empirical grounds. The only ultimately defensible politics is, therefore, one in which such challenges are continuously and openly possible. Limitations of Kohlberg's (or any other system's) view of morality are a problem only to the extent that their provisions are used to justify coercive practices, especially the coercion of discourse. As will become apparent, the political practices outlined in the next section are not thus employed.

3. The desire for cultural relativity seems to arise from a concern that genetic-epistemological theories might devalue human beings. However, moral philosophers distinguish two forms of moral judgments: "deontic" judgments of moral obligation and "aretaic" judgments of moral worth (Frankena, 1963:8–10). Genetic-epistemological theories concern only deontic judgments: empirically, such theories demonstrate how deontic judgments develop; philosophically, they argue that later judgments are preferable (scientifically, morally, or aesthetically, depending on the domain) to earlier judgments.

People misinterpret genetic epistemology as an attempt to categorize people as better or worse (whether in intelligence, morality, or just plain value as human beings). According to this misunderstanding, genetic epistemology allows people who reason at a given stage to rule (at best) or to denigrate, dismiss, or silence (at worst) those reasoning at lower stages.

Unfortunately, the belief that genetic epistemology justifies aretaic judgments is found not just among genetic epistemology's critics but also among those who accept its cognitive-developmental framework of developmental sequences, structural stages, and so on. For example, Suzi Gablik (1977) misunderstands the larger implications of genetic epistemology in her otherwise illuminating attempt to understand art history from a cognitive-developmental perspective. Briefly, Gablik argues that the history of painting over the past several thousand years reveals the Piagetian developmental sequence of decreasing egocentrism and increasing coordination of viewpoints. Today's children are thus closer artistically to artists of two thousand years ago than they are to present-day adult artists. Her argument, supported by numerous historical examples, appears unexceptionable; the examples are clear, and the interpretation is plausible.

The problem, however, lies in the title of the book itself: *Progress in Art*. The implicit claim is that modern art is better art,[10] but Gablik fails to provide philosophical grounds for this aesthetic claim. The claim of a developmental sequence in artistic representation is an empirical claim, but the claim that higher is better is a philosophical claim requiring a separate justification. As with the so-called "naturalistic fallacy" in moral philosophy,[11] one cannot reach conclusions of aesthetic value by empirical arguments alone.[12]

Despite these misunderstandings by both supporters and critics of genetic epistemology, its theories provide no basis for aretaic judgments. As Kohlberg puts it (1984:324):

> I explicitly state that my stage theory is not a theory claiming to aretaically grade individuals or cultures on some scale of moral worthiness. . . . Deontic judgments of rightness are more adequate and more likely to lead to consensus at Stage 5 or 6,

but this does not mean that I assume that a morally conscientious and consistent actor using Stage 4 deontic reasoning to guide his actions is to be assigned lesser moral worth on some aretaic scale I explicitly say I do not have.[13]

In U.S. culture, deontic judgments are confused with aretaic judgments: to condemn someone's reasoning is to condemn that person. It is easy to see how this confusion would arise, since one's survival here depends on being "right." As a worker, to think accurately is to be assured of continuing employment and thus money for food, health coverage, and so on. As a citizen, to know and agree with U.S. cultural doctrines is to enjoy the respect of one's fellow citizens and (in the final analysis) to stay out of jail.

This identification of deontic and aretaic judgments is not inevitable, however. One can make intellectual judgments without personal condemnation, even indirect personal condemnation through loss of job and income, etc. In fact, there appears to be no rational basis for any aretaic judgment of humans.[14] As noted earlier in the discussion of deontic and aretaic judgments, genetic epistemology evaluates the moral adequacy or persuasiveness of moral judgments of rights and obligations; it does not evaluate the worth of the people making the judgments.[15]

The lack of aretaic judgments does not obviate discourse over development, however. The genetic-epistemological perspective is rooted in deontic judgments—in the present case, judgments of cultural practices. Discussions of development require deontic critique of cultural practices, but such discussions need not assert aretaic judgments of those practices' practitioners.

4. Because Kohlberg's work drives *DPD*'s macro-level theory of political development, his comments would appear particularly damning, especially since Kohlberg always showed a determined nicety about what philosophical implications his work would and would not support. However, for two reasons— one trivial, the other deep—Kohlberg's objections do not apply to *DPD*'s extension of his work to political development. Trivially, his objections do not apply because the extension does not use average moral maturity scores to classify cultures. Instead, I use the concept of political culture, defined as "all publicly common ways of relating," to enable analysts to stage-score a culture independently of its members' stage scores.[16]

But clearly this is the flimsiest of defenses: Kohlberg is objecting to the use of stage scores in *any* form to evaluate cultural practices. A deeper response to the objections is as follows: the developmental hierarchy of cultures is not an evaluation of the moral worth of the cultures (that is, not an aretaic judgment of them) but instead an evaluation of the reasons by which cultural organization and practices are justified (that is, a deontic judgment). Kohlberg himself recognizes the possibility of evaluating cultural practices, as he states in the sentences elided from those quoted above:

> However, our agreement with relativism in this sense does not require us as moral agents to adopt an ethically relativistic position and so claim, for example, that Aztec human sacrifice is right. While it is true that the principles compatible with

postconventional reasoning would lead one not to endorse the Aztec practice of human sacrifice, such a judgment constitutes a moral evaluation of a specific cultural practice, not of a culture per se (Kohlberg, 1984:331).

In *DPD* I frame the issue in terms of the distinction between structure and content:

> [This theory of] development does not require a culture to become like any more-developed culture, but instead requires that each culture resolve the structural ambiguities of its current stage in its own fashion. Even though there is a culturally universal sequence of organizing structures, there is no universal sequence of specific social forms (*DPD*, pp.75–76).

In other words, the stage-structural analysis of a culture allows us to recognize, through our knowledge of each structure's inherent ambiguities, the types of oppression to which a culture might be prone. Cultures relying upon Stage 4 reasoning, for example, will have difficulty dealing with other cultures or with internal dissent. To say this is not to condemn any particular culture; it is possible (if unlikely) that a culture has no dissenters and never comes into contact with any other culture. The theory gives no basis for condemning this fortunate culture for its practices; the theory only notes areas in which difficulties may arise. However, the theory does assert a natural duty for searching out those excluded from normative discourse.

Moreover, even a culture facing difficulties (e.g., a Stage 4 culture facing internal dissent or external contact) deserves no aretaic reproach for the practices by which it attempts to end its difficulties. We can condemn the practices, but it is clear that the members of the culture (or the culture as a whole, if one can speak meaningfully of such a thing) are doing the best they can, given their current intellectual resources and the situation facing them. Choice lies in the future. Because genetic epistemology recognizes that developmental change is always possible, it is not a framework by which to reproach people for the dead past.

III.   The Political Practice Implied By Genetic Epistemology

This section lays out the various aspects of social organization, and particularly political practice, that appear to flow from the perspective of genetic epistemology. It deals with two aspects of politics: the nature of politics in a genetic-epistemologically oriented society and how development should be fostered. This section does not present a complete vision of political life, however; it concentrates instead on those aspects of politics to which genetic epistemology seems directly applicable.

A.   *General Political Goals Implied by Genetic Epistemology*

Open Discourse.   The root of genetic epistemology is its view of develop-ment as originating in a process of "equilibration" between subject and object. At the most general level of abstraction—what Piaget saw as the biological basis of his paradigm—two functions underlie all life: organization and adaptation. Life is organized and attempts to adapt to its environment. Adaptation can take place through either of two functions (or both simultaneously): assimilating the environment to the organism's current organization, or accommodating the organization to the environment. Specific examples of assimilation include (in biology) chewing and digesting the environment, which reduces the complexity of the physical world to the category of food, and (in cognition) seeing every human interaction as an opportunity to make a buck, which reduces the complexity of the social world to the category of "marks." Specific examples of accommodation include (in biology) the development of teeth and jaws and salivary glands, which enable the organism to process a wider variety of food, and (in cognition) the development of different techniques to con different kinds of marks. In general, knowledge is constituted in the organization of an organism equilibrated to its environment.

Because the social world is constituted by language (and other symbolic communication), we need to look at what equilibration means in that domain. As Habermas has shown, language, and thus social life itself, is possible only when every utterance implicitly carries a series of validity claims: that the utterance is comprehensible, that its propositional content about the real world is true, that its expression of the speaker's experience is authentic, and that the utterance is right within the social context shared by the parties to it. This last claim is essentially a *moral* claim: a statement that the moral universe within which the discourse is occurring makes sense from all the points of view involved. Moral reasoning has to do with the structure of mutual understandings and obligations in terms of which people make sense of their social action. Thus, from a genetic-epistemological perspective, an equilibrated moral position is one that is equally justified from every point of view in the moral relationship under consideration. In the moral domain, equilibration means that one's view of the moral issues involved does not change in response to different perspectives or in response to nonmoral alterations in the situation. "Different perspectives" means how moral questions look to different people (or to the same person under different but morally identical circumstances).[17]

The redemption of the different validity claims requires different means. Claims to objective truth require a philosophy of science; claims to self-revelation require psychoanalytic inquiry, etc. The present work is particularly concerned with the redemption of moral claims, that is, with the claim that the social actors participating in a relationship agree on its morality. To establish this claim requires open discourse among the various parties, and thus every moral claim must be acknowledged—indeed, sought out! Far from silencing people, genetic-epistemological politics demands a careful, equal, and complete attention to everyone's voice.

The necessity for "equal and complete" consideration may not be apparent; why isn't it sufficient to give merely "careful" consideration to everyone? This requirement arises from genetic epistemology's view of equilibration: a cognitive structure is equilibrated only if it is consonant with all possible perspectives. It is not equilibrated if it holds merely for the majority of perspectives, or for most of the perspectives, or usually: only for all, and all the time.

Such consideration of different perspectives has meaning only on the assumption that we can understand them. After all, if we cannot understand others' points of view, we cannot equilibrate our concerns with theirs. Genetic epistemology is therefore founded on the assumption that, as Terence said, "Nothing human is alien to me." Discourse is possible not just between closely related individuals but also between actors whose cultures differ widely from one another. The assumption is that we are not condemned, ultimately, to merely strategic action. Strategic action may be employed as part of the ordinary conduct of life, or when our practical resources for discourse fail, but genetic epistemology assumes that the ground of our social existence is always open to meaningful, discursive challenge. This assumption is not susceptible to direct proof or disproof, of course, but it seems plausible that if discourse is possible within close relationships, it is possible within all. The gaps in understanding between two closely tied people differ only in degree from those between any two people. Granted, the less experience that people share, the more obstacles their discourse will encounter, but this would seem to be a problem only of time and determination, not an existential barrier to human relationships.

Genetic epistemology also implies an active search for, and honoring of, different perspectives. Genetic-epistemological politics is ceaselessly aware of the possibility that perspectives may differ, that our equilibrated social agreements will have broken down between one moment and the next. We all occasionally have social interactions in which an unsuspected gap in understanding or belief suddenly opens up before us. Genetic-epistemological politics treats such circumstances as an opportunity for discourse oriented to reestablishing a fuller understanding, not as a signal for strategic action to impose one's own perspective. The first fundamental requirement of genetic-epistemological politics, therefore, is the creation of forums and techniques to facilitate such discourse.

The Elimination of Hegemonic Limitations on Discourse. In practice, of course, our own or others' experience and understanding are regularly denied through a variety of means. People are oppressed directly: incarcerated or killed so that their views are not heard, or threatened so they are afraid to express them, or denied access to the public forum (Parenti, 1978, 1986). People are segregated from one another, so that one group is denied access to the other's perspective.[18] People are oppressed "internally," so that they come to deny the validity of their own experience (Lipsky, 1987). People are isolated from others with similar experience, so that little opportunity for social validation or development of their voice occurs. People are kept without the conceptual, linguistic, and discursive tools to express their understandings (Fraser, 1986).[19] Ideologies purport to prove the validity claims of a political system but simultaneously resist any examination of the discourse basis under which such claims are considered (Marcuse, 1965; Habermas, 1975:112–113).

Overcoming such practical difficulties is the second requirement of genetic-epistemological politics. As asserted in the previous chapter, we require a critical praxis that is both consistent with the precepts of genetic epistemology and effective against existing institutional and internalized oppressions. Our task as theorists is no longer solely theoretical; ultimately, we have to learn how to apply our universal truths in our own contexts—to learn, ourselves, and to teach others. Such a practical subject is where this work leaves off, however; my concern in the present work remains theoretical and philosophical. But having acknowledged the importance of the demand for such a praxis, I do want to indicate two general considerations for it.

First, it is clear that open discourse is only possible when all people have equal access to the public forum. This would seem to require relative equality among people's financial and educational resources.[20] Many different arrangements might ensure such relative equality; I will merely note that Rawls (1971: esp. Sections 33, 36, and 43) presents a sketch of one such arrangement.

"Equal access to the public forum" means a positive public obligation to ensure that all people have the resources necessary to participate in the public forum. It seems to me that the major advance since John Locke in our theoretical understanding has been our recognition that the classical liberal freedom to participate—i.e., the mere absence of legal barriers—is insufficient to maintain open discourse. Marxists and, more recently, feminists have pointed out hegemonic processes distorting liberal discourse. Their respective emphases on the class and gender lines of hegemony sufficiently illustrate the existence of hegemonic forces, in my view, but by no means exhaust our analysis. Indeed, I would argue that our deepening perception of hegemonic forces and our developing invention of ways to surmount them are never-ending processes.

Second, our quest to establish equal access to the public forum cannot rest with institutional reform. The hegemonic forces cited above do not derive solely from unjust institutions, that is, from strategic considerations of effective individual action within a given institutional framework, even assuming that the participants are aware of the nature of the oppression. Hegemonic forces also arise from oppression supported by erroneous beliefs held by members of the oppressed class themselves and from the very language within which claims are pressed. Since these institutional and internalized oppressions reinforce one another, the creation of a just society requires dealing with both simultaneously. Just institutions may be able to "generate their own support" (Rawls, 1971:177), but it seems unlikely that they can create support where none existed before. Some "pedagogy of the oppressed" (Friere, 1970) is clearly required.

Even leaving aside issues of internalized oppression, no set of institutions addresses all hegemonic forces forever. As in life itself, organization is always subject to developmental adaptation under the pressure of equilibration. In the social world, every institutional solution to existing hegemonies creates its own practical limits on discourse, thus requiring further development to pay heed to still-ignored perspectives.[21] Genetic-epistemological politics rejects the idolatry of any institutional solution and takes as its ultimate values only discourse itself and the emancipation arising therefrom.

Punishment and the Separation of Deontic and Aretaic Judgments.   Although I argued earlier that genetic epistemology provides no basis for aretaic judgments, punishment would seem to be an exception to that. The legal process of formal charges, trial, and punishment seems specifically intended to establish an aretaic judgment of the accused: a judgment of that person's value as a member of society and the physical expression of that judgment. Certainly the common prejudice against former convicts is an aretaic judgment. Apparently, then, a society that punishes people—which, ignoring utopian fantasies, would seem to mean *any* society—is, at least in that respect, engaged in aretaic judgment. If this were so, then genetic-epistemological politics, denying such judgments, could only be seen as an impossible utopianism.

It is possible, however, to assert a theory of punishment free of aretaic judgment. Following Rawls (1971:240, Section 39), one can view punishment as merely a practice to ensure everyone's confidence in others' willingness to adhere to the just institutions.[22] This shifts the focus of concern away from aretaic judgments of the accused's value as a member of society and towards deontic judgments of whether her reasons for action are legitimate. It also shifts the assessment of punishment away from a focus on the miscreant's evilness (or to revenge); instead, punishment is assessed according to broader principles of social justice weighing a continuing respect for the accused's liberty against the loss of liberty to all (including the accused) arising from lack of punishment. Thus even for the domain of punishment, where one might think aretaic judgment would certainly be involved, genetic epistemology offers no hold for aretaic judgments about people's comparative value.[23] Each individual's value is absolute, even though the value of her vagrant wishes and reasons is not; people always have reasons that appear good to them to act as they do.

The refusal to make aretaic judgments is easily confused with certain "value neutral" or "value relativist" positions, whose adherents may easily conclude that genetic epistemology implies no basis for holding anyone to any contract. But this is a misunderstanding; while value relativism rejects the evaluation of both people and reasons, genetic epistemology only rejects the evaluation of people. One can evaluate people's reasons for their moral choices as more or less adequate, without implying that they are bad people for holding those reasons. In fact, the genetic-epistemological perspective is unavoidably concerned with those processes of discourse through which people broaden and refine their reasoning.

The Nature of Respect for Reasoning at Different Levels.   Genetic epistemology's psychological requirement of equilibration implies all people's claim to be heard, subject to their respect for others' like claims. From this point of view, genetic epistemology seems to provide no basis for paternalistic denial of people's equal rights. At the same time, its deontic evaluation of different arguments seems to provide a definite basis for ignoring "lower-stage" arguments. How is this apparent contradiction to be resolved?[24]

1. Under no circumstances can one restrict people's claim to be respected as persons, meaning their right to have their basic ("categorical") moral claims respected. A genetic-epistemological recognition that a person's arguments are not well cast has nothing to do with her implicit claims as a human being to just treatment. Categorical claims apply to all.

2. Under no circumstances can one restrict people's claim to equal consideration of their contingent ("hypothetical") interests, as long as such interests do not violate categorical imperatives.[25] Even if our arguments for our ends are not well cast, we deserve respect as human beings trying to forward our interests.

3. From the standpoint of genetic epistemology, cognitive development arises not from a passive acquiescence to some externally defined truth but rather from the active process of construction that occurs during the equilibration of the world and one's cognitive structures. It follows that under no circumstances can we restrict thinking and that we are justified in restricting actions only when they present a clear and present danger to the just claims of actors or of others. "The question of equal liberty of conscience is settled. It is one of the fixed points of our considered judgments of justice" (Rawls, 1971:206).[26]

4. Any inequality in the degree of attention given to competing arguments or in the degree of access available to desired positions must be justified on one of two grounds: (1) that an individual's reasoning, if followed, or occupancy of a position, if allowed, would violate the categorical imperative to give equal respect to everyone's moral claims; or (2) that an individual's reasoning (or occupation of a position) is inadequate to ensure her own good. Criterion (2) must be applied only charily, however, since it is subject to several problems. First, paternalism deprives people of the very experience necessary for them to observe the effects of their action and to modify it accordingly, or to occupy a position and learn its requirements. Only a very serious and direct threat to a person's well-being (e.g., preventing a child from running into a busy street) or a firm knowledge that the experience would not produce knowledge (e.g., for someone brain-damaged), can warrant a restriction of that person's experience. Second, we must recognize that no person can totally appreciate the rich, personal significance of another's aims. It is easy to make one's own distaste or misunderstanding into a speciously universalistic judgment about others' choice in an original position. Paternalism is notoriously employed to disguise exploitation, and one need not even assume exploitation to recognize that it is all too easy to assume that one's own ends are everyone's.

5. In *DPD*, pp.84–86, I assert that, other things being equal, regimes will

tend to be more just, legitimate, and stable when political rank is proportional to moral reasoning stage. The problem of moral imperialism obviously arises.[27] The above points (1–4) show to what extent one would favor such rule. It is easiest to frame the issue in the Rawlsian terms of what would be agreed to in an original position. *DPD*'s analysis points to certain aspects of cognitive psychology, communication patterns, and political activity that affect the ability of a regime to be just and, by retaining legitimacy, stable. These considerations would, it seems to me, be admitted into the original position as part of what Rawls (1971:137) terms "general facts about... political affairs,.. social organization and the laws of human psychology." These considerations would not affect the choice of principles of justice, I think, but would affect the choice among constitutions.

It is certainly possible that justice would *not* be served—liberty not protected and enhanced, or the least well-off position not advanced—by distinguishing people on the basis of moral reasoning level. Such distinctions may come to have aretaic connotations that make them marks of separation and inferiority, even if those connotations are not supported by the theory that creates the distinctions.[28] If so, then justice would demand that they not be recognized. Such concerns are both serious and legitimate and thus require careful attention. Properly understood, genetic epistemology does not force us to make distinctions that do not advance justice.

B.   The Development Support
Policy Implied by Genetic Epistemology

Being a developmental theory itself, genetic epistemology surely has lessons for how societies should support one another's development.[29] Many of the remarks below are unfortunately vague—mere guidelines when we would like clear decision rules—but guidelines are all that a general treatment like this can reasonably establish. In addition, I restrict myself to those considerations of development policy that arise from genetic epistemology. The important issue of when intervention is justified therefore remains unaddressed, because the complex questions it raises seem to me little illuminated by strictly genetic-epistemological considerations.

Anybody Can Play.   We first return to the theme of distinguishing deontic and aretaic judgments. Like people, societies are free to critique the policies and practices of other societies: to note contradictions and make suggestions. Such deontic judgments of other societies' reasoning should stop short of aretaic judgments of blame and condemnation. The latter sort of judgments accomplish nothing except the degradation of relations. If we start with the assumption that every person is doing the best she can within the limits of her moral understanding and political power, then there can be no grounds for the aretaic judgments implicit in reproofs and reproaches.

Note also that criticisms by "more-developed" societies are not privileged; no society is above challenge. It may happen that society X, employing reasoning at a lower cognitive stage than that of society Y, may find it hard to challenge Y's beliefs. Regardless of this difficulty, Y still faces the necessity of taking X's perspective into account. Earlier I said that genetic epistemology implies an honoring of different perspectives. Honoring here does not mean remaining slavishly neutral toward others' perspectives, of course, but it does mean coming to grips with them. Our politics ought to allow us neither to dismiss others without full consideration nor to leave them in error if they are wrong.

Definite But Reasonable Expectations.   The general difficulty of cognitive development, particularly for a culture collectively, implies that we must have reasonable expectations for societies' development. This applies to both the problems we point out and the policies we suggest. Societies will not change stages overnight, and impatience is politically futile, not to mention forgetful of the Western world's prolonged and bloody developmental struggles.

This is not to propose a passivity of purpose on our part; we can still speak clearly and strongly about developmental challenges other countries face. It is, however, to suggest that we measure in clearer developmental terms the progress made against the progress we expect, and that we acknowledge, praise, and encourage measurable developmental advances, not merely criticize failures or inaction.

Distinguish Development from National Security Policy.   A *development* policy is best targeted at developing moral reasoning, not at eliciting pro–United States attitudes, or trade concessions, or military bases. A nation's ability to maintain an effective development policy will certainly depend on its own security, so these attitudes, concessions, and bases have their place. We must recognize, however, that a development policy has goals separate from such considerations—including, in particular, the goal of eliminating hegemonic control.

The Cultural Relativism of Developmental Resolutions.   Even if two cultures are at different developmental levels, development policy does not require that the less-developed culture become like the more-developed. Cognitive development only occurs when reasoners find and resolve ambiguities and contradictions within their own cognitive structure. Societal development therefore depends on a culture's widespread recognition of its own ambiguities and contradictions. Other countries' institutions may provide appropriate solutions to such problems, but the primary criterion of a development policy must be cultural appropriateness. Any other criterion simply reflects an exercise of hegemonic control. *Development* policy fosters indigenous developmental resolutions to a culture's indigenous problems; it does not impose particular (read: Western) institutions.

As a consequence, development policy should aid indigenous and progressive movements, not alien, regressive, or repressive movements. Development policymakers must take ideologies more seriously as reflecting the emergence into consciousness of certain cultural contradictions. This consciousness cannot be suppressed without moral violence; it would appear that the best we can do is stay out of the gears while they turn. Support of reactionary, repressive regimes against strong, popular movements pointing out real problems is short-sighted and unconscionable. Policymakers may gain a decade or so of stable repression, but their country loses its international reputation and, ultimately, its self-respect as an agent of development.

The issue is not whether we should refuse any connection with repressive governments; clearly there will be situations in which there is no reasonable alternative. The true issue is rather whether we are capable of abandoning such alliances when popular opposition to the government crystallizes.

C.   *Conclusion*

My major concern in this work, particularly in this final chapter and more particularly in the description of genetic-epistemological politics, has been that the conceptualization of development presented in *DPD* be both *coherent* as a theoretical approach to the study of development and *realistic* as a practical model for development. In other words, I have tried to demonstrate that the approach to development advanced here and in *DPD* is useful to both my academic and political colleagues.

I have tried to advance only arguments deriving from the genetic-episte-mological perspective. The connection of this perspective with the later chapters (5–9) is clear, because these chapters discuss social processes whose dynamics arise from moral reasoning development, but the connection with the earlier, theoretical chapters (2–4) appears more subtle. For example, Chapter 2's lengthy discussion of the analytical method may seem to be far removed from Piaget and Kohlberg. Nevertheless, genetic epistemology and the analytical method are closely connected through their central concern with equilibration. Genetic epistemology sees development (including cognitive development) as driven by the need to coordinate different frames of reference, so that the organism's structure (cognitive structure) can maintain itself in its environment without the need for structural change. In the domain of moral development, equilibration means stability of the moral framework regardless of the actor. Similarly, the analytical method seeks to establish a theoretical framework that is invariant across people, so that different people agree on the framework used. The process of discourse in the domain of the analytical method is similar to that found in the domain of morality; in both cases, people make universal claims, reflect those claims against others' perspectives, and advance general criteria to resolve conflicts. In short, I see both the specifics of my conceptualization of political development and the analytical method through which I justify it as arising from the same underlying approach, an approach rooted in mutual respect for others' perspectives and practiced through open discourse.

Notes

1. Good overviews or illustrations of the genetic-epistemological perspective can be found in Flavell (1963), Kohlberg (1981, 1984), Parsons (1987), and Piaget (1970).

2. The perception that elements take their meaning from their location within a larger context is not unique to genetic epistemology, of course. It is shared by the nonstructuralist Gestalt psychologists (e.g., Koffka, 1935) and by structuralists like Levi-Strauss (1963) and Chomsky (1975).

3. Thus an early stage provides object permanence: one recognizes that objects exist even if they are taken out of sight. At such elementary levels, of course, the structures are coordinations of physical operations rather than of the internal representations of actions we come to call "thought."

4. Thus, for example, the Stage 4 structure allows one to uphold a common set of laws regardless of one's personal affiliations.

5. Vygotsky (1978) may provide the basis for another constructivist, interactionist theory. In comparison with Kohlberg's theory, however, Vygotsky's stages are much less clearly elaborated and their normative ground is not well established.

6. Chapter 5, n.33. The empirical results cited in the text currently apply only to Kohlberg's scoring system, which embraces judgments of justice, not of morality as a whole. I discuss later the implications of this limitation; suffice it here to say that whatever the failings of Kohlberg's specific formulation, a suitably revised version would not alter the present argument.

7. See also Kohlberg's (1984:217ff.) careful exposition of this relationship between philosophy and psychology, which he elaborated in response to Habermas's (1983) suggestions.

8. Piaget recognized the role of social interaction in psychological development, but he did not speak of a development of macro social structures corresponding to the sequence of cognitive structures.

9. This chapter concentrates on philosophical rather than methodological criticisms of Kohlberg's work. Kohlberg's most recent scoring system and the validity studies of it have answered the methodological objections, I believe; many of these objections arose from earlier formulations of the theory and scoring system.

The first three sets of criticisms below are taken from Shweder (1982), Simpson (1974), Sullivan (1977), Gilligan (1977, 1982), Gilligan and Murphy (1979), and Murphy and Gilligan (1980). The last set of criticisms appears in Kohlberg (1981, 1984).

10. One might infer an additional claim that historically later artists are better artists. Such evaluation seems pointless, however. Clearly, every artist does the best she can within the historical situation she encounters (materials, styles, tutors, and schools of thought, not to mention personal difficulties). In classical Greece an Einstein might have discovered ideas of great value, but not the theory of relativity!

11. An argument makes the naturalistic fallacy when it attempts to derive moral conclusions solely from empirical premises. See Kohlberg (1981:101–189).

12. Gablik does not specifically address this implication of her title. Michael J. Parsons's (1987) discussion of a developmental sequence of aesthetic judgment provides some philosophical support for the implicit claim of Gablik's title, even though Parsons does not cite Gablik's work.

13. The deontic-aretaic distinction also applies to the domains of science and

aesthetics. In those domains, deontic judgments become judgments of the *adequacy of standards* of proof (science) or of aesthetic value (aesthetics). Aretaic judgments become those of the *value* of a discovery or a career (science) or of a work of art or an artist (aesthetics).

14. As Harvey Jackins (1981) has put it:

> Every single human being, when the entire situation is taken into account, has always, at every moment of the past, done the very best that he or she could do, and so deserves neither blame nor reproach from anyone, including self. This, in particular, is true of you (by permission of Rational Island Publishers).

15. Indeed, Kohlberg holds that Stage 6 reasoning assigns equal moral worth to every human being.

16. Simple aggregation of individual characteristics cannot define the characteristics of a society; this is the well-known problem of the "micro–macro connection." I raise this problem explicitly both in *DPD* and in Chapter 5 of this book. But even though Kohlberg's comments are not appropriate to the conception of stage scoring I employ, they must be examined to see if they might still apply.

17. The preceding two sentences appear circular: one decides what a "moral" argument is by seeing if it excludes "nonmoral" circumstances. If this definition were indeed circular, it would be meaningless. However, the self-reference becomes successive approximation and not circularity. This issue is central to a class of works employing the very similar concepts of equilibration (Piaget), dialectical reasoning (Marx), reflective equilibrium (Rawls), critical theory (Habermas), etc. Habermas (1975:109–117) explicates the logic behind this apparent circularity.

18. Class stratification patterns in residence and education, for example, result in little contact between members of different economic, ethnic, or racial groupings. Thus, members of each grouping are relatively free to propound moral positions oppressive to the other grouping—and even to employ such positions, to the extent that it is within their power to do so.

19. See the material from Fraser (1986:425) quoted in Chapter 8, note 4. Friere (1970) makes a similar point.

20. It would also seem to require relative equality among corporations, since the latter are inevitably influential in establishing cultures conducive to their own products.

21. Some institutions will be better than others, of course. It is possible that a utopia might eventually exist in which all perspectives receive full respect. But the statement that we cannot rest with any given structure certainly seems valid for the foreseeable future!

22. "Others" in this case would include people who don't grasp the justice of the institutions and the consequent obligation to obey them. For an argument that Rawls in fact provides no justification for punishment, see Brubaker (1988:829–831).

23. It might appear that Rawls (1971: Section 66) makes aretaic judgments in his theory of good applied to persons, in which he states the sort of virtues we rationally would like people to have: "the broadly based features of moral character that it is rational for the persons in the original position to want in one another" (p.437). However, the evaluations implied by this view of the good are not linked to people's right to liberty, distributive shares, or moral treatment in general. Saying what virtues it is rational to want people to possess is not the same as condemning people for failing to possess them.

24. The following discussion draws largely on Rawls (1971: esp. Sections 37 and 40).

25. In other words, we are bound to respect everyone's pursuit of their own ends, limited only by those universalizable considerations that would be accepted in an initial position occupied by free and equal rational beings. These limitations are of two types.

First, the ends themselves can be judged rational or not. Thus Tommy's ambition to be the greatest pinball player in the world would be admissible, however odd it was, since it violated no one else's basic rights; but Hitler's ambition to kill the Jews would not be admissible, since it contemplated the violation of the prior, categorical right of Jews to life. Second, ends that are reasonable in small degrees can be limited by principles of justice that address the cumulative effect of these ends on others. Thus the ownership of property for personal use might be acceptable, while unlimited acquisition might be rejected as harmful to the least well off.

26. It is therefore an argument for the genetic-epistemological perspective that it provides firm ground for liberty of conscience, and that it does so using an argument independent of Rawls's. In other words, the considerations adduced by genetic epistemology are not simply those of Rawls translated into a different language.

27. For example, Palmer (1989) sees my genetic-epistemological orientation as the latest form of Plato's rule by the elite, defining the elite as the highest stage reasoners.

28. We must also recognize the possibility that such difficulties will vary according to the society concerned. This is why I believe that the idea of developmental distinctions would not arise until Rawls's "constitutional convention" stage, where the occupants of the original position acquire some idea of the nature of the society to which their constitutional arrangements will apply.

29. Several of these points also appear in *DPD*, pp.109–111.

Bibliography

Almond, Gabriel (1956) "Comparative Political Systems" *Journal of Politics* 18:391–409.

_____ (1973) "Approaches to Developmental Causation" in Almond, Flanagan, and Mundt (eds) (1973:1–42).

Almond, Gabriel, Scott Flanagan, and Robert Mundt (eds) (1973) *Crisis, Choice and Change: Historical Studies of Political Development* (Boston: Little, Brown).

Almond, Gabriel, and G. Bingham Powell (1966) *Comparative Politics: A Developmental Approach* (Boston: Little, Brown).

Almond, Gabriel, and Sidney Verba (1963) *The Civic Culture: Political Attitudes and Democracy in Five Nations* (Boston: Little, Brown).

_____ (eds) (1980) *The Civic Culture Revisited* (Boston: Little, Brown).

Aronoff, Joel (1967) *Psychological Needs and Cultural Systems* (Princeton, NJ: Van Nostrand).

_____ (1970) "Psychological Needs as a Determinant in the Formation of Economic Structures: A Confirmation" *Human Relations* 23:123–138.

Arrow, Kenneth (1951) *Social Choice and Individual Values* (New York: Wiley).

Babbie, Earl (1986) *The Practice of Social Research* (Belmont, CA: Wadsworth).

Benhabib, Seyla (1986) "The Generalized and the Concrete Other: The Kohlberg–Gilligan Controversy and Feminist Theory" *Praxis International* 5:402–424.

Bensel, Richard Franklin (1984) *Sectionalism and American Political Development 1880–1980* (Madison: University of Wisconsin Press).

Bernstein, B. (1966) "Elaborated and Restricted Codes: Their Social Origins and Some Consequences" in A. Smith (ed), *Communication and Culture* (New York: Holt, Rinehart and Winston).

Berti, Anna Emilia, Anna Silvia Bombi, and Rossana De Bene (1986) "Acquiring Economic Notions: Profit" *International Journal of Behavioral Development* 9:15–29.

Berti, Anna Emilia, Anna Silvia Bombi, and Adriana Lis (1982) "The Child's Conceptions about Means of Production and Their Owners" *European Journal of Social Psychology* 12:221–239.

Bertilson, H., D. Springer, and K. Fierke (1982) "Underrepresentation of Female Referents as Pronouns, Examples and Pictures in Introductory College Textbooks" *Psychological Reports* 51:923–931.

Blasi, Augusto (1980) "Bridging Moral Cognition and Moral Action: A Critical Review of the Literature" *Psychological Bulletin* 88:1–45.

Bondurant, Joan V. (1971) *Conquest of Violence: The Gandhian Philosophy of Conflict* (Berkeley: University of California Press).

Brown, Archie, and Jack Gray (eds) (1977) *Political Culture and Political Change in Communist States* (New York: Holmes and Meier).

Brown, Archie (1977) "Introduction" in Brown and Gray (eds) (1977).

_____ (ed) (1984) *Political Culture and Communist Studies* (Armonk, NY: M. E. Sharpe).

Brubaker, Stanley C. (1988) "Can Liberals Punish?" *American Political Science Review* 82:821–836.

Bunch, Ralph (1971) "Orientational Profiles: A Method for Micro–Macro Analysis of Attitude" *Western Political Quarterly* 24:666–674.

Candee, Dan, and Lawrence Kohlberg (1983) "Moral Reasoning and Obedience to Authority" (Unpublished monograph, Graduate School of Education, Harvard University).

_____ (1984) "Moral Judgment and Moral Action: A Reanalysis of Haan, Smith, and Block's FSM Study" in W. Kurtines and A. Gewirth (eds), *Morality, Moral Behavior, and Moral Development* (New York: Wiley).

Carnap, Rudolph (1950) *Logical Foundations of Probability* (Chicago: University of Chicago Press).

Charlesworth, James C. (ed) (1967) *Contemporary Political Analysis* (New York: Free Press).

Chilton, Stephen (1977) *The Analysis of Power Structures in Three High Schools* (Unpublished Ph.D. dissertation, Cambridge, MA: Massachusetts Institute of Technology).

_____ (1984) "Non-Survey Methods of Political Culture Research" (Typescript).

_____ (1988a) "Any Complete Theory of Social Change Inevitably Incorporates a Normatively Grounded Theory of Moral Choice" *Journal of Developing Societies* 4:135–148.

_____ (1988b) *Defining Political Development* (Boulder: Lynne Rienner Publishers).

Chomsky, Noam (1975) *Reflections on Language* (New York: Pantheon).

Colby, Ann, and Lawrence Kohlberg (1987) *The Measurement of Moral Judgment* (2 Volumes) (New York: Cambridge University Press).

Colby, Ann, Lawrence Kohlberg, John Gibbs, and Marcus Lieberman (1983) "A Longitudinal Study of Moral Judgment" *Monographs of the Society for Research in Child Development* (1, Serial No. 200).

Coleman, James S. (1973) *The Mathematics of Collective Action* (Chicago: Aldine).

Cuthbertson, G. M. (1975) *Political Myth and Epic* (Lansing, MI: Michigan State University Press).

Damon, William (ed) (1978) *New Directions for Child Development: Moral Development* 2.

Danet, Brenda (1971) "The Language of Persuasion in Bureaucracy: 'Modern' and 'Traditional' Appeals to the Israel Customs Authorities" *American Sociological Review* 36:847–859.

Dittmer, Lowell (1977) "Political Culture and Political Symbolism: Toward a Theoretical Synthesis" *World Politics* 29:552–583.

Dobelstein, Andrew W. (1985) "The Bifurcation of Social Work and Social Welfare: The Political Development of Social Services" *Urban and Social Change Review* 18:9–12.

Douglas, Mary (1982) *In the Active Voice* (Boston: Routledge and Kegan Paul).

Dowding, Keith M., and Richard Kimber (1983) "The Meaning and Use of 'Political Stability'" *European Journal of Political Research* 11: 229–243.

Eberhardt, Nancy (1984) *Knowledge, Beliefs and Reasoning: Moral Development and Culture Acquisition in a Shan Village of Northern Thailand* (Unpublished Ph.D. dissertation, Urbana, IL: University of Illinois at Champaign–Urbana).

Eckstein, Harry (1982) "The Idea of Political Development: From Dignity to Efficiency" *World Politics* 34:451–486.

Edelman, Murray (1964) *The Symbolic Uses of Politics* (Urbana: University of Illinois Press).

Edwards, Carolyn (1975) "Societal Complexity and Moral Development: A Kenyan Study" *Ethos* 3:505–527.

Edwards, David V. (1989) "Theorizing As Practice: Raising Our Theoretical Consciousness" (Paper presented at the annual meeting of the American Political Science Association, Atlanta).

Elazar, Daniel (1966) *American Federalism: A View from the States* (New York: Crowell).

_____ (1970) *Cities of the Prairie* (New York: Basic Books).

Elder, Charles D., and Roger W. Cobb (1983) *The Political Uses of Symbols* (New York: Longman).

Fishkin, James (1982) *Beyond Subjective Morality* (New Haven: Yale University Press).

Flavell, John H. (1963) *The Developmental Psychology of Jean Piaget* (New York: Van Nostrand).

_____ (1968) *The Development of Role-Taking and Communication Skills in Children* (New York: Wiley).

Foley, Michael (1986) *The Languages of Contention: Political Language, Moral Judgement, and Peasant Mobilization in Contemporary Mexico* (Unpublished Ph.D. dissertation, Davis, CA: University of California at Davis).

Ford, M. R., and C. R. Lowery (1986) "Gender Differences in Moral Reasoning: A Comparison of the Use of Justice and Care Orientations" *Journal of Personality and Social Psychology* 50:777–783.

Foster, Charles (1982) "Political Culture and Regional Ethnic Minorities" *Journal of Politics* 44:560–568.

Frankena, William K. (1963) *Ethics* (Englewood Cliffs, NJ: Prentice-Hall).

Fraser, Nancy (1986) "Toward a Discourse Ethic of Solidarity" *Praxis International* 5:425–429.

_____ (1989) "Struggle over Needs: Outline of a Socialist–Feminist Critical Theory of Late-Capital Political Culture" (Paper presented at the annual meeting of the American Political Science Association, Atlanta).

Frey, Frederick W. (1963) "Political Development, Power, and Communications in Turkey" in Pye (ed) (1963:Chapter 17).

Friere, Paulo (1970) "Pedagogy of the Oppressed" in Charles K. Wilbur (ed), *The Political Economy of Development and Underdevelopment* (4th edition) (New York: Random House).

Gablik, Suzi (1977) *Progress in Art* (New York: Rizzoli).

Gallie, W. B. (1956) "Essentially Contested Concepts" *Proceedings of the Aristotelian Society* 56(n.s.):167–198.

Gaus, Gerald (1990) *Value and Justification* (New York: Cambridge University Press).

Geertz, Clifford (1973) *The Interpretation of Cultures* (New York: Basic Books).

_____ (1984) "Distinguished Lecture: Anti Anti-Relativism" *American Anthropologist* 86:263–278.

Gibbs, John (1977) "Kohlberg's Stages of Moral Judgment: A Constructive Critique" *Harvard Educational Review* 47:43–61.

Gilligan, Carol (1977) "In a Different Voice: Women's Conceptions of Self and Morality" *Harvard Educational Review* 47:481–517.

_____ (1982) *In a Different Voice: Psychological Theory and Women's Development* (Cambridge: Harvard University Press).

Gilligan, Carol, and J. M. Murphy (1979) "Development from Adolescence to Adulthood: The Philosopher and the 'Dilemma of the Fact'" in Deanna Kuhn (ed), *Intellectual Development Beyond Childhood* (San Francisco: Jossey-Bass).

Greenberg, Edward (1970) "Children and Government: A Comparison Across Racial

Lines" *Midwest Journal of Political Science* 14:249–275.

Habermas, Jüergen (1975) *Legitimation Crisis* (Boston: Beacon Press).

_____ (1979) *Communication and the Evolution of Society* (Boston: Beacon Press).

_____ (1979a) "What is Universal Pragmatics?" in Habermas (1979:Chapter 1).

_____ (1983) "Interpretive Social Science vs. Hermaneuticism" in Norma Haan et al. (eds), *Social Science as Moral Inquiry* (New York: Columbia University Press).

Hagen, Everett (1962) *On the Theory of Social Change: How Economic Growth Begins* (Homewood, IL: Dorsey).

Hallpike, Christopher Robert (1979) *Foundations of Primitive Thought* (Oxford: Oxford University Press).

Hempel, Carl G. (1952) *Concept Formation in Empirical Science* (Chicago: University of Chicago Press).

Hess, Robert D., and Judith V. Torney (1967) *The Development of Political Attitudes in Children* (Chicago: Aldine).

Hewitt, John P. (1979) *Self and Society: A Symbolic Interactionist Social Psychology* (2nd edition) (Boston: Allyn and Bacon).

Higgins, E. Tory, Diane Ruble, and Willard Hartup (1983) *Social Cognition and Social Development: A Sociocultural Perspective* (New York: Cambridge University Press).

Hill, David (1981) "Political Culture and Female Political Representation" *Journal of Politics* 43:159–168.

Hobhouse, Lawrence Trelawney (1906) *Morals in Evolution* (London: Chapman and Hall).

Holsti, K. J. (1975) "Underdevelopment and the 'Gap' Theory of International Conflict" *American Political Science Review* 69:827–839.

Hoover, Kenneth R. (1984) *The Elements of Social Scientific Thinking* (3rd edition) (New York: St. Martin's).

Hope, Kempe Ronald (1985) "Electoral Politics and Political Development in Post-independence Guyana" *Electoral Studies* 4:57–68.

Hudelson, Richard (1990) *Marxism and Philosophy in the Twentieth Century: A Defense of Vulgar Marxism* (New York: Praeger).

Huntington, Samuel (1965) *Political Order in Changing Societies* (New Haven, CT: Yale University Press).

_____ (1971) "The Change to Change: Modernization, Development, and Politics" *Comparative Politics* 3:283–322.

Jackins, Harvey (1981) *The Benign Reality* (Seattle: Rational Island Publishers).

Jaros, D., H. Hirsch, and Frederick J. Fleron (1968) "The Malevolent Leader: Political Socialization Within an American Subculture" *American Political Science Review* 62:564–575.

Jennings, M. Kent, and Richard G. Niemi (1974) *The Political Character of Adolescence* (Princeton: Princeton University Press).

Johnson, Charles A. (1976) "Political Culture in American States: Elazar's Formulation Examined" *American Journal of Political Science* 20:491–509.

Jowitt, Kenneth (1974) "An Organizational Approach to the Study of Political Culture in Marxist-Leninist Systems" *American Political Science Review* 68:1171–1191.

Kavanagh, Dennis (1972) *Political Culture* (New York: Macmillan).

Khalilzad, Zalmay (1984–5) "The Politics of Ethnicity in Southwest Asia: Political Development or Political Decay?" *Political Science Quarterly* 99:657–679.

Kim, Young (1964) "The Concept of Political Culture in Comparative Politics" *Journal of Politics* 26:313–336.

Koffka, K. (1935) *Principles of Gestalt Psychology* (New York: Harcourt, Brace).

Kohlberg, Lawrence (1981) *Essays on Moral Development: Vol. I. The Philosophy of Moral Development* (San Francisco: Harper and Row).

_____ (1984) *Essays on Moral Development: Vol. II. The Psychology of Moral*

Development (San Francisco: Harper and Row).

_____ (1984a) "Stage and Sequence: The Cognitive-Developmental Approach to Socialization" in Kohlberg (1984).

Kohlberg, Lawrence, Charles Levine, and Alexandra Hewer (1984a) "The Current Form of the Theory" in Kohlberg (1984).

_____ (1984b) "Synopses and Detailed Replies to Critics" in Kohlberg (1984).

Lehman, Edward (1972) "On the Concept of Political Culture: A Theoretical Reassessment" *Social Forces* 50:361–370.

Lerner, Daniel (1958) *The Passing of Traditional Society* (Glencoe, IL: The Free Press).

Levi–Strauss, Claude (1963) *Structural Anthropology* (New York: Basic Books).

Lichter, L., and S. Lichter (1983) *Prime Time Crime: Criminals and Law Enforcers in TV Entertainment* (Washington: The Media Institute).

Lipsky, Suzanne (1987) *Internalized Racism* (Seattle: Rational Island).

Long, Samuel L. (ed) (1981) *The Handbook of Political Behavior. Volume 4* (New York: Plenum Press).

Lowery, David, and Lee Sigelman (1982) "Political Culture and State Public Policy: The Missing Link" *Western Political Quarterly* 35:376–384.

Marcuse, Herbert (1965) "Repressive Tolerance," in Wolff, Robert Paul, Barrington Moore, Jr., and Herbert Marcuse (eds), *A Critique of Pure Tolerance* (Boston: Beacon Press), pp. 81–117.

McAuley, Mary (1984) "Political Culture and Communist Politics: One Step Forward, Two Steps Back" in Brown (1984).

McClelland, David (1976) *The Achieving Society* (New York: Irvington).

McMillian, J., and S. Ragan (1983) "The Presidential Press Conference: A Study in Escalating Institutionalization" *Presidential Studies Quarterly* 12:231–241.

Mead, George Herbert (1962) *Mind, Self, and Society* (Chicago: University of Chicago Press).

Medhurst, M. (1977) "American Cosmology and the Rhetoric of Inaugural Prayer" *Central States Speech Journal* 28:272–282.

Metzger, Thomas A. (1981) Preface, in Wilson, Greenblatt, and Wilson (1981).

Miller, J. (1984) "Political Culture: Some Perennial Questions Reopened" in Brown (1984).

Moreno, Jacob Levy (1934) *Who Shall Survive? A New Approach to the Problem of Human Interactions* (Washington, DC: Nervous and Mental Disease Publishing Company).

Murphy, J. M., and Carol Gilligan (1980) "Moral Development in Later Adolescence and Adulthood: A Critique and Reconstruction of Kohlberg's Theory" *Human Development* 23:77–104.

Nimmo, Dan, and James E. Combs (1983) *Mediated Political Realities* (New York: Longman).

Nisan, Mordacai, and Lawrence Kohlberg (1984) "Cultural Universality of Moral Judgment Stages: A Longitudinal Study in Turkey" in Kohlberg (1984:582–593).

Overton, Willis F. (1983) *The Relationship Between Social and Cognitive Development* (Hillsdale, NJ: Erlbaum).

Palmer, Monte (1989) *Dilemmas of Political Development* (4th edition) (Itasca, IL: F. E. Peacock Publishers).

Parenti, Michael (1978) *Power and the Powerless* (New York: St. Martin's Press).

_____ (1986) *Inventing Reality: The Politics of the Mass Media* (New York: St. Martin's Press).

Park, Han S. (1984) *Human Needs and Political Development* (Cambridge, MA: Schenkman).

Parsons, Michael J. (1987) *How We Understand Art: A Cognitive Developmental Account of Aesthetic Experience* (New York: Cambridge University Press).

Parsons, Talcott (1961) "An Outline of the Social System" in Parsons et al. (eds) (1961).

Parsons, Talcott, and Edward Shils (eds) (1951) *Toward a General Theory of Action: Theoretical Foundations for the Social Sciences* (New York: Harper and Row).

Parsons, Talcott, Edward Shils, Kaspar D. Naegele, and Jesse R. Pitts (eds) (1961) *Theories of Society: Foundations of Modern Sociological Theory* (New York: The Free Press).

Pateman, Carol (1971) "Political Culture, Political Structure and Political Change" *British Journal of Political Science* 1:291–305.

_____ (1980) "The Civic Culture: A Philosophic Critique" in Almond and Verba (1980).

Payne, James L. (1984) *Foundations of Empirical Political Analysis* (second printing) (College Station, TX: Lytton).

Piaget, Jean (1932) *The Moral Judgment of the Child* (New York: Free Press).

_____ (1970) *Structuralism* (New York: Basic Books).

_____ (1977) *Etudes Sociologique* (Geneva: Librairie Droz).

Power, Clark, and Joseph Reimer (1978) "Moral Atmosphere: An Educational Bridge Between Moral Development and Action" in Damon (ed) (1978).

Putnam, Robert (1976) *The Comparative Study of Political Elites* (Englewood Cliffs, NJ: Prentice-Hall).

Pye, Lucian W. (ed) (1963) *Communications and Political Development* (Princeton: Princeton University Press).

_____ (1966) *Aspects of Political Development* (Boston: Little, Brown).

_____ (1966a) "The Concept of Political Development" in Pye (1966:Chapter 2).

_____ (1972) "Culture and Political Science: Problems in the Evaluation of the Concept of Political Culture" *Social Science Quarterly* 10:285–296.

Radding, Charles M. (1978) "Evolution of Medieval Mentalities: A Cognitive-Structural Approach" *American Historical Review* 83:577–597.

_____ (1979) "Superstition to Science: Nature, Fortune, and the Passing of the Medieval Ordeal" *American Historical Review* 84:945–969.

_____ (1985) *A World Made by Men: Cognition and Society, 400–1200* (Chapel Hill, NC: University of North Carolina Press).

Rawls, John (1971) *A Theory of Justice* (Cambridge, MA: Belknap Press).

_____ (1985) "Justice As Fairness: Political Not Metaphysical" *Philosophy and Public Affairs* 14:223–251.

Raz, Joseph (1990) "Facing Diversity: The Case of Epistemic Abstinence" *Philosophy and Public Affairs* 19:3–46.

Rest, James (1973) "The Hierarchical Nature of Moral Judgment" *Journal of Personality* 41:86–109.

Riggs, Fred W. (1967) "The Theory of Political Development" in Charlesworth (1967:317–349).

_____ (1981) "The Rise and Fall of 'Political Development" in Long (1981:Chapter 6).

Rosenberg, Shawn, Dana Ward, and Stephen Chilton (1988) *Political Reasoning and Cognition: A Piagetian View* (Durham: Duke University Press).

Rosenwasser, M. (1969) "Six Senate War Critics and Their Appeals for Gaining Audience Response" *Communications Quarterly* 17:43–50.

Scheuch, Erwin (1967) "Society as Context in Cross-Cultural Comparisons" *Social Science Information* 6:7-23.

_____ (1968) "The Cross-Cultural Use of Sample Surveys: Problems of Comparability" in Stein Rokkan (ed), *Comparative Politics Across Cultures and Nations* (Paris and The Hague: Mouton).

Scott, James C. (1976) *The Moral Economy of the Peasant* (New Haven, CT: Yale University Press).

_____ (1985) *Weapons of the Weak: Everyday Forms of Peasant Resistance* (New

Haven, CT: Yale University Press).

Selman, Robert (1971) "The Relation of Role–Taking to the Development of Moral Judgment in Children" *Child Development* 42:79–91.

Shafir, M. (1983) "Political Culture, Intellectual Dissent, and Intellectual Consent: The Case of Romania" *Orbis* 27:393–420.

Shorter, E., and Charles Tilly (1974) *Strikes in France 1830–1968* (New York: Cambridge University Press).

Shweder, Richard (1982) Review of Lawrence Kohlberg's *Essays on Moral Development: Volume I The Philosophy of Moral Development*, in *Contemporary Psychology* 27:421–424.

Simpson, Elizabeth Leonie (1974) "Moral Development Research: A Case Study of Scientific Cultural Bias" *Human Development* 17:81–106.

Sinclair, K. (1982) "British Prestige Press Editorials on Readership During 1979 Campaign" *Journalism Quarterly* 59:230–234ff.

Smith, Tony (1985) "Requiem or New Agenda for Third World Studies?" *World Politics* 37:532–561.

Snarey, James, Joseph Reimer, and Lawrence Kohlberg (1984) "Cultural Universality of Moral Judgment Stages: A Longitudinal Study in Israel" in Kohlberg (1984:594–620).

Sollie, Finn (1984) "Polar Politics: Old Games in New Territories, or New Patterns in Political Development?" *International Journal* 39:695–720.

Stone, Clarence N. (1980) "Systemic Power in Community Decision Making: A Restatement of Stratification Theory" *American Political Science Review* 74:978–990.

Sullivan, Edmund V. (1977) "A Study of Kohlberg's Structural Theory of Moral Development: A Critique of Liberal Social Science Ideology" *Human Development* 20:352–376.

Szalay, Lorand B., and Rita Mae Kelly (1982) "Political Ideology and Subjective Culture: Conceptualization and Empirical Assessment" *American Political Science Review* 76:595–602.

Thompson, E. P. (1971) "The Moral Economy of the English Crowd in the Eighteenth Century" *Past and Present* 50:76–136.

Tilly, Charles (1978) *From Mobilization to Revolution* (Reading, MA: Addison-Wesley).

Turiel, Elliot (1966) "An Experimental Test of the Sequentiality of Developmental Stages in the Child's Moral Judgment" *Journal of Personality and Social Psychology* 3:611–618.

Vaillancourt, Pauline Marie (1986) *When Marxists Do Research* (Westport, CT: Greenwood Press).

Van Dijk, T. (1983) "Discourse Analysis: Its Development and Application to the Structure of News" *Journal of Communication* 33:20–43.

Vygotsky, Lev (1978) *Mind in Society* (Cambridge, MA: Harvard University Press).

Walker, Lawrence J. (1982) "Sex Differences in the Development of Moral Reasoning: A Critical Review of the Literature" (Paper presented at the Canadian Psychological Association, Montreal).

Weber, Max (1958) *The Protestant Ethic and the Spirit of Capitalism* (New York: Charles Scribner's Sons).

Weiner, Myron, and Samuel P. Huntington (eds) (1987) *Understanding Political Development* (Boston: Little, Brown).

Weinreich, Helen (1977) "Some Consequences of Replicating Kohlberg's Original Moral Development Study on A British Sample" *Journal of Moral Education* 7:32–39.

Wellhofer, E. Spencer (1989) "The Comparative Method and the Study of Development, Diffusion, and Social Change" *Comparative Political Studies* 22:315–342.

Weschler, Lawrence (1989) "A Reporter at Large (Uruguay—Part I)" *The New Yorker* 65:43–85.

White, Lynn, Jr. (1962) *Medieval Technology and Social Change* (New York: Oxford University Press).

Williamson, Judith (1978) *Decoding Advertisements* (London: Marion Boyars).

Wilson, Edmund O. (1975) *Sociobiology: The New Synthesis* (Cambridge, MA: Belknap Press).

Wilson, Richard, Sidney Greenblatt, and Amy Auerbacher Wilson (1981) *Moral Behavior in Chinese Society* (New York: Praeger).

Wolin, Sheldon (1960) *The Politics of Vision: Continuity and Innovation in Western Political Thought* (Boston: Little, Brown).

Yeager, F. (1974) "Linguistic Analysis of Oral Edited Discourse" *Communications Quarterly* 22:29–36.

Index

Agreement on conceptions and FTRs, 1, 4, 9, 11, 12, 14–18, 20, 22, 39, 58, 116

Almond, Gabriel: Almond (1956), 15, 57, 59, 62, 81, 82, 93, 121; Almond (1973), 33, 121; Almond and Powell (1966), 60, 81, 121; Almond and Verba (1963), 15, 57, 58, 62, 65, 81, 82, 87, 89, 91, 92, 121; Almond and Verba (1980), 82, 121; Almond, Flanagan, and Mundt (1973), 121

Analytical method, 1, 4, 5, 7, 11–22, 58–61, 116; undercut by extratheoretical forces, 9, 13, 21. *See also* Hegemony and hegemonic forces

Aretaic judgments of moral worth, 84, 104, 106–108, 112, 114, 117, 118. *See also* Deontic judgments of moral obligation and validity

Aronoff, Joel: Aronoff (1967), 54, 84, 121; Aronoff (1970), 84, 121

Arrow, Kenneth: Arrow (1951), 22, 121

Artistic/aesthetic development. *See* Development, artistic/aesthetic

Babbie, Earl: Babbie (1986), 13, 121

Benhabib, Seyla: Benhabib (1986), 96, 97, 105, 121

Bensel, Richard Franklin: Bensel (1984), 2, 121

Bernstein, B.: Bernstein (1966), 83, 121

Berti, Anna Emilia: Berti, Bombi, and De Bene (1986), 83, 121; Berti, Bombi, and Lis (1982), 83, 121

Bertilson, H.: Bertilson, Springer, and Fierke (1982), 74, 121

Blasi, Augusto: Blasi (1980), 76, 121

Bombi, Anna Silvia: Berti, Bombi, and De Bene (1986), 83, 121; Berti, Bombi, and Lis (1982), 83, 121

Bondurant, Joan V.: Bondurant (1971), 40, 121

Brown, Archie: Brown (1977), 61, 64, 83, 121; Brown (1984), 122, 125; Brown and Gray (1977), 61, 64, 121

Brubaker, Stanley C.: Brubaker (1988), 118, 122

Bunch, Ralph: Bunch (1971), 81, 122

Candee, Dan: Candee and Kohlberg (1983), 76, 122; Candee and Kohlberg (1984), 76, 122

Carnap, Rudolph: Carnap (1950), 21, 122

Change (in contrast to development), 3, 4, 9, 13, 24, 27–33, 35–40, 44, 92. *See also* Development; Political development

Change/e theories, 28, 29, 35–38, 40, 41

Change/i theories, 28, 33–35, 40

Change/n theories, 29, 36–38, 40, 41

Charlesworth, James C.: Charlesworth (1967), 122, 126

Chilton, Stephen: Chilton (1977), 92, 122; Chilton (1984), 84, 122; Chilton (1988a), 92, 122; Chilton (1988b), 1, 4–8, 14, 23, 24, 26, 27, 29, 37, 39, 41, 43, 44, 46, 80, 84, 85, 92, 95, 99, 101, 103, 107, 108, 113, 114, 116, 118, 119, 122; Rosenberg, Ward, and Chilton (1988), 36, 92, 103, 126

Chomsky, Noam: Chomsky (1975), 83, 117, 122

Cobb, Roger W.: Elder and Cobb (1983), 82, 123

Cognitive development, 6, 8, 58, 73, 76, 79, 80, 83–85, 103, 105, 106, 108, 109, 112–117

Cognitive structure, 24, 44, 58, 66, 71–74, 76–80, 84, 103, 109, 113, 115–117; cleavages in, 6

Colby, Ann: Colby and Kohlberg (1987), 8, 84, 101, 122; Colby et al. (1983), 72, 83, 84, 122

Coleman, James S.: Coleman (1973), 40, 122

Combs, James E.: Nimmo and Combs (1983), 82, 125

Conceptual pluralist position on conceptualization, 20. *See also* Unitary position on conceptualization

Conservative social science, 38, 39. *See also*

Emancipatory social science
Cultural relativity and cross-cultural validity, 9, 15, 19, 20, 46, 53, 57, 60–66, 71–73, 75, 76, 78, 81, 84, 104, 106, 107, 112, 115
Culture. See Political culture
Cuthbertson, G. M.: Cuthbertson (1975), 82, 122

Damon, William: Damon (1978), 122, 126
Danet, Brenda: Danet (1971), 72, 122
De Bene, Rossana: Berti, Bombi, and De Bene (1986), 83, 121
Defining Political Development (Chilton, 1988b), 1, 4–8, 14, 23, 24, 26, 27, 29, 37, 39, 41, 43, 44, 46, 80, 84, 85, 92, 95, 99, 101, 103, 107, 108, 113, 114, 116, 118, 119, 122
Deontic judgments of moral obligation and validity, 11, 29, 33, 84, 87, 88, 105–107, 109, 110, 112–114, 117. See also Aretaic judgments of moral worth
Development: artistic/aesthetic, 106, 117; of biological organisms and/or species, 24, 26, 32–35, 45, 102, 108, 109; economic, 2, 6, 8; social, 6. See also Change; Modernization; Political development; Progress; Westernization
Dittmer, Lowell: Dittmer (1977), 58–61, 65–67, 75, 81–83, 122
Dobelstein, Andrew W.: Dobelstein (1985), 2, 122
Douglas, Mary: Douglas (1982), 83, 122
Dowding, Keith M.: Dowding and Kimber (1983), 20, 122

Eberhardt, Nancy: Eberhardt (1984), 84, 122
Eckstein, Harry: Eckstein (1982), 7, 23, 49, 51–55, 122
Economic development. See Development, economic
Edelman, Murray: Edelman (1964), 82, 122
Edwards, Carolyn: Edwards (1975), 73, 123
Edwards, David V.: Edwards (1989), 40, 123
Elazar, Daniel, 61–63, 82, 124; Elazar (1966), 62, 123; Elazar (1970), 62, 63, 123
Elder, Charles D.: Elder and Cobb (1983), 82, 123
Emancipatory social science, 34, 38, 39, 98, 112. See also Conservative social science
Empirical theories of normative choice. See Change/e theories
Ethnocentrism and moral imperialism, 13, 28, 39, 50, 65, 104, 106, 107, 113, 114, 119
Exact specification. See Fundamental theoretical requirements, of exact specification

Feminist criticisms: of Kohlberg, 83, 99, 104–107; of Rawls (etc.), 8, 96–100, 111. See also Benhabib; Fraser; Gilligan; Hegemony and hegemonic forces
Fierke, K.: Bertilson, Springer, and Fierke (1982), 74, 121
Fishkin, James: Fishkin (1982), 83, 123
Flanagan, Scott: Almond, Flanagan, and Mundt (1973), 121
Flavell, John H.: Flavell (1963), 103, 117, 123; Flavell (1968), 83, 123
Fleron, Frederick J.: Jaros, Hirsch, and Fleron (1968), 82, 124
Foley, Michael: Foley (1986), 30, 123
Ford, M. R.: Ford and Lowery (1986), 99, 123
Foster, Charles: Foster (1982), 82, 123
Frankena, William K.: Frankena (1963), 106, 123
Fraser, Nancy: Fraser (1986), 96, 97, 99, 105, 110, 118, 123; Fraser (1989), 54, 123
Freudianism and psychoanalysis, 33, 34, 109
Frey, Frederick W.: Frey (1963), 92, 123
Friere, Paulo: Friere (1970), 39, 111, 118, 123
Fruitfulness of conceptions, 4, 9, 12, 14, 15, 17, 18, 20, 79, 81
Fundamental theoretical requirements (FTRs): acceptance of, 17, 18; in analytical method, 1, 4, 5, 9, 14–22, 54; competing conceptions and, 19; completeness of range of, 18; of development beyond current societies, 44, 46; of exact specification, 23–26, 49, 51, 53, 54; exclusion of all conceptions by, 19; of humans as locus of development, 45–47; of ideal type definition, 43, 44, 46; justification of, 23–41; of laws of development, 43, 46; of the locus of development, 23, 54; metacriteria for, 16, 17, 46, 47; of the micro–macro connection, 23, 26, 27, 50, 52–55; of normative grounding, 23, 27–41, 50, 52–55; for political culture, 16, 22, 58–66, 70, 71, 75, 76, 78, 81–83; for political development, 1, 4–7, 9, 16, 17, 23–54; proposed by other theorists, 43–47, 53; of the recognition of development, 23, 24, 50, 52, 55; reflective equilibrium, 19; sources of, 15, 16; of teleological development, 45; of universal applicability, 44–46. See also Agreement on conceptions and FTRs

Gablik, Suzi: Gablik (1977), 106, 117, 123
Gallie, W. B.: Gallie (1956), 3, 123
Gandhi, Indira, 54
Gandhi, Mohandas, 34, 40, 121

Gaus, Gerald: Gaus (1990), 96, 123
Geertz, Clifford: Geertz (1973), 40, 60, 61,
    65, 66, 67, 76, 77, 83, 123; Geertz (1984),
    84, 123
Genetic epistemology: political practice of,
    101–119
Gibbs, John: Colby et al. (1983), 73, 83, 84,
    122; Gibbs (1977), 83, 123
Gilligan, Carol, 6, 121; Gilligan (1977), 117,
    123; Gilligan (1982), 83, 96, 99, 105, 117,
    123; Gilligan and Murphy (1979), 117,
    123; Murphy and Gilligan (1980), 117,
    125
Grau, Craig, 9
Gray, Jack: Brown and Gray (1977), 64, 121
Greenberg, Edward: Greenberg (1970), 82,
    123
Greenblatt, Sidney: Wilson, Greenblatt, and
    Wilson (1981), 125, 128

Habermas, Jürgen, 21, 33; Habermas (1975),
    33, 83, 111, 118, 123; Habermas (1979),
    33, 41, 83, 97, 98, 109, 123; Habermas
    (1979a), 11, 87, 88, 124; Habermas
    (1983), 83, 105, 117, 124
Hagen, Everett: Hagen (1962), 25, 124
Hallpike, Christopher Robert: Hallpike
    (1979), 78, 124
Hanson, Russell, 15
Hartup, Willard: Higgins, Ruble, and Hartup
    (1983), 83, 124
Hegel, 9
Hegemony and hegemonic forces, 8, 21, 69,
    80, 82, 103, 110–112, 115. See also
    Analytical method, undercut by
    extratheoretical forces; Feminist criticisms
Hempel, Carl G.: Hempel (1952), 5, 8, 13, 21,
    124
Hess, Robert D.: Hess and Torney (1967), 85,
    102, 124
Hewer, Alexandra: Kohlberg, Levine, and
    Hewer (1984a), 73; Kohlberg, Levine, and
    Hewer (1984b), 83, 105, 125
Hewitt, John P.: Hewitt (1979), 65, 81–83,
    124
Higgins, E. Tory: Higgins, Ruble, and Hartup
    (1983), 83, 124
Hill, David: Hill (1981), 82, 124
Hirsch, H.: Jaros, Hirsch, and Fleron (1968),
    82, 124
Hobbes, Thomas, 11, 96
Hobhouse, Lawrence Trelawney: Hobhouse
    (1906), 29, 40, 124
Holsti, K. J.: Holsti (1975), 44, 124
Hoover, Kenneth R.: Hoover (1984), 13, 124
Hope, Kempe Ronald: Hope (1985), 2, 124

Hudelson, Richard: Hudelson (1990), 40, 124
Huntington, Samuel: Huntington (1965), 40,
    124; Huntington (1971), 3, 9, 11, 20, 24,
    37, 39, 124; Weiner and Huntington
    (1987), 2, 8, 9, 127

Impersonal theories of normative choice. See
    Change/i theories

Jackins, Harvey: Jackins (1981), 118, 124
Jaros, D.: Jaros, Hirsch, and Fleron (1968),
    82, 124
Jefferson, Thomas, 54
Jennings, M. Kent: Jennings and Niemi
    (1974), 82, 124
Johnson, Charles A.: Johnson (1976), 82, 124
Jowitt, Kenneth: Jowitt (1974), 61, 63, 64,
    124

Kant, Immanuel, 22, 90
Kavanagh, Dennis: Kavanagh (1972), 59, 61,
    62, 81, 124
Kelly, Rita Mae: Szalay and Kelley (1982),
    82, 127
Khalilzad, Zalmay: Khalilzad (1984–1985), 2,
    124
Kim Il-Sung, 54
Kim, Young: Kim (1964), 81, 124
Kimber, Richard: Dowding and Kimber
    (1983), 21, 122
King, Martin Luther, Jr., 34
Koffka, K.: Koffka (1935), 117, 124
Kohlberg, Lawrence, 6, 8, 16, 37, 73, 74, 77,
    79, 80, 83, 84, 99, 101–105, 107, 116–
    118, 121, 123; Candee and Kohlberg
    (1983), 76, 122; Candee and Kohlberg
    (1984), 76, 122; Colby and Kohlberg
    (1987), 8, 84, 101, 122; Colby et al.
    (1983), 73, 83, 84, 122; Kohlberg (1981),
    36, 41, 73, 83, 84, 87, 96–99, 101, 103,
    104, 107, 117, 118, 124; Kohlberg (1984),
    36, 84, 87, 96–99, 101, 105–107, 117,
    118, 124; Kohlberg (1984a), 73, 83, 84,
    103, 124, 125; Kohlberg, Levine, and
    Hewer (1984a), 73, 83, 84, 125; Kohlberg,
    Levine, and Hewer (1984b), 83, 105, 125;
    Nisan and Kohlberg (1984), 73, 74, 125;
    Snarey, Reimer, and Kohlberg (1984), 73,
    74, 127
Kohlberg's scoring system, 8, 74, 84, 99,
    104–106, 117, 118. See also Colby and
    Kohlberg (1987)

Lehman, Edward: Lehman (1972), 21, 59, 60,
    77, 81, 125
Lerner, Daniel: Lerner (1958), 32, 125

Levi-Strauss, Claude, 83; Levi-Strauss (1963), 117, 125
Levine, Charles: Kohlberg, Levine, and Hewer (1984a), 73, 83, 84, 125; Kohlberg, Levine, and Hewer (1984b), 83, 105, 125
Lichter, L.: Lichter and Lichter (1983), 74, 125
Lichter, S.: Lichter and Lichter (1983), 74, 125
Lieberman, Marcus: Colby et al. (1983), 73, 83, 84, 122
Lipsky, Suzanne: Lipsky (1987), 110, 125
Lis, Adriana: Berti, Bombi, and Lis (1982), 83, 121
Locus of development: culture as the, 7, 23, 87–93; FTR of, 23, 43. *See also* Fundamental theoretical requirements, of the locus of development
Long, Samuel L.: Long (1981), 125, 126
Lowery, C. R.: Ford and Lowery (1986), 99, 123
Lowery, David: Lowery and Sigelman (1982), 82, 125

Marcuse, Herbert: Marcuse (1965), 111, 125
Marx and Marxist thought, 9, 29, 40, 55, 61, 82, 100, 111, 118
McAuley, Mary: McAuley (1984), 60, 125
McClelland, David, 54; McClelland (1976), 74, 84, 87, 89, 92, 125
McMillian, J.: McMillian and Ragan (1983), 74, 125
Mead, George Herbert: Mead (1962), 32, 125
Medhurst, M.: Medhurst (1977), 74, 125
Metzger, Thomas A.: Metzger (1981), 36, 125
Micro–macro connection. *See* Fundamental theoretical requirements, of the micro–macro connection
Miller, John: Miller (1984), 81, 125
Modernization. *See* Political development
Moral considerations of choice, 31–38. *See also* Practical considerations of choice
Moral density, 52
Moral development, 6–8, 29, 36, 37, 40, 50, 51, 72, 73, 76, 79, 80, 83, 84, 87, 89, 99, 101–105, 107, 114–116. *See also* Political development
Moral imperialism. *See* Ethnocentrism and moral imperialism
Moral reasoning, 6–8, 27–29, 31–41, 44, 53, 69, 72–77, 79, 80, 83, 84, 87, 89, 95, 96, 98, 99, 101–105, 107, 109, 112, 114–116
Moral relationship with others, 95–97, 99, 105, 109. *See also* Ways of relating and the ways of relating perspective
Morality, 27, 29, 31–41, 51, 53, 72, 74, 75,

77, 80, 84, 88, 90, 95, 96, 98, 99, 102–107, 110, 112–114, 116–118
Moreno, Jacob Levy: Moreno (1934), 90, 125
Mundt, Robert: Almond, Flanagan, and Mundt (1973), 121
Murphy, J. M.: Gilligan and Murphy (1979), 117, 123; Murphy and Gilligan (1980), 117, 125

Naegele, Kaspar D.: Parsons et al. (1961), 125
Niemi, Richard G.: Jennings and Niemi (1974), 82, 124
Nimmo, Dan: Nimmo and Combs (1983), 82, 125
Nisan, Mordecai: Nisan and Kohlberg (1984), 73, 74, 125
Normative grounding. *See* Fundamental theoretical requirements, of normative grounding
Normatively grounded theories of normative choice. *See* Change/n theories

Operationalization, 2, 8, 12, 13, 15, 43, 57; difficulty of is irrelevant, 4, 5, 12, 17
Overton, Willis F.: Overton (1983), 83, 125

Palmer, Monte: Palmer (1989), 40, 119, 125
Parenti, Michael: Parenti (1978), 110, 125; Parenti (1986), 110, 125
Park, Han S., 43; Park (1984), 2, 7, 43–47, 49–54, 125
Parsons, Michael J., 102; Parsons (1987), 117, 125
Parsons, Talcott, 68, 81, 87, 102; Parsons (1961), 32, 126; Parsons and Shils (1951), 87, 126; Parsons et al. (1961), 125
Pateman, Carol: Pateman (1971), 61, 62, 70, 81, 126; Pateman (1980), 70, 126
Payne, James L.: Payne (1984), 8, 13, 126
Piaget, Jean, 6, 8, 36, 46, 58, 71–74, 83, 102, 104, 109, 116–118, 123, 126; Piaget (1932), 83, 126; Piaget (1970), 83, 117, 126; Piaget (1977), 83, 126
Pitts, Jesse R.: Parsons et al. (1961), 126
Political culture, 6–8, 12, 13, 15, 20, 24, 26, 27, 36, 41, 46, 47, 53, 57–85, 110, 118; Almond's definition of, 57, 62, 82; Almond and Verba's definition of, 57, 58, 61–66, 70, 78, 82; Brown's definition of, 61, 64, 78, 83; Chilton's definition of, 6–8, 22–24, 27, 46, 47, 57, 58, 66–71, 75–81; cognitive structure underlying, 58, 66, 71–74, 76–80, 83, 84, 103, 104, 108, 115; comparability of across political systems, 59–61, 64–66, 71, 76, 78, 79, 81, 104, 105, 108, 115; confusion over definition

of, 57–59, 75, 78, 81; content-structure distinction in, 73, 76–80, 84, 85, 108; contrasted with economic culture, 75; contrasted with physical culture, 81; Dittmer's definition of, 61, 65–67, 78, 83; Elazar's definition of, 61–63, 78, 82; fundamental theoretical requirements of definition of, 58–61, 78; Jowitt's definition of, 61, 63, 64, 78; as locus of development, 7, 23, 46, 87–93; measurement of, 60, 64, 73–75, 79–81; as mediating the micro–macro connection, 27, 59, 81, 103; moral development stage scoring of, 8, 72–76, 83, 84, 103–108; role of in explanation, 76–78, 80–82; subcultures, 61, 62, 68, 79, 80; use of analytical method in, 14–17, 19, 21, 58–61, 78. See also Public commonness; Sharedness of culture

Political development, 1, 2, 4–9, 11–17, 19, 21, 23–25, 41, 43, 46, 78, 80, 95, 99, 101, 103, 107, 108, 111, 116, 117; applicability to all societies of, 44; beyond current societies, 44–46; Chilton's definition of, see Chilton (1988b); connection between micro and macro facets of, 26, 27, 50, 52, 53, 103, 117; dynamics of, 7, 25, 53, 70, 80, 84, 85, 103; Eckstein's conception of, 49, 51–55; exact specification of, 24–26, 50, 51, 53; humans as the locus of, 45, 46; ideal-type definition of, 43, 44; laws of, 43; locus of, 7, 23, 39, 50, 52, 87–93; multiplicity and confusion of definitions of, 1–4, 8, 9, 20, 24, 39; nonexistence of concept of, 3, 4, 8, 9, 20; normative grounding of, 24, 27–40, 50, 51, 53; Park's conception of, 49–51, 53–55; policy fostering, 101, 108, 114–116; recognition of, 24, 40, 50, 52; in the sense of mere change, 2, 24, 39; as a teleological process, 24, 39, 45; use of analytical method in, 7. See also Change; Modernization; Moral development; Progress; Westernization

Portis, Edward, 83

Powell, G. Bingham: Almond and Powell (1966), 60, 81, 121

Power, Clark: Power and Reimer (1978), 36, 126

Practical considerations of choice, 31. See also Moral considerations of choice

Progress, 9, 38, 41, 45, 46, 50, 106. See also Political development

Public commonness, 27, 47, 66, 68–71, 74, 76, 79, 81, 85, 107. See also Political culture; Sharedness of culture

Putnam, Robert: Putnam (1976), 59, 82, 126

Pye, Lucian W.: Pye (1963), 32, 123, 126; Pye (1966), 126; Pye (1966a), 2, 9, 12, 25, 126; Pye (1972), 61, 66, 77, 81, 126

Radding, Charles M., 78; Radding (1978), 78, 84, 126; Radding (1979), 74, 78, 84, 126; Radding (1985), 29, 36, 41, 126

Ragan, S.: McMillian and Ragan (1983), 74, 125

Rawls, John, 16, 19, 96, 118; Rawls (1971), 16, 19, 21, 53, 96–99, 111–114, 118, 119, 126; Rawls (1985), 98, 126

Raz, Joseph: Raz (1990), 98, 126

Recognition of development. See Fundamental theoretical requirements, of the recognition of development

Reimer, Joseph: Power and Reimer (1978), 36, 126; Snarey, Reimer, and Kohlberg (1984), 73, 74, 127

Reptiles as moral reasoners, 2, 36, 41

Rest, James: Rest (1973), 84, 126

Riggs, Fred W.: Riggs (1967), 8, 126; Riggs (1981), 2, 3, 11, 20, 126

Rightness. See Validity claims, of rightness

Rosenberg, Shawn: Rosenberg, Ward, and Chilton (1988), 36, 92, 103, 126

Rosenwasser, M.: Rosenwasser (1969), 74, 126

Ruble, Diane: Higgins, Ruble, and Hartup (1983), 83, 124

Scheuch, Erwin: Scheuch (1967), 60, 62, 126; Scheuch (1968), 60, 62, 81, 126

Scott, James C.: Scott (1976), 33, 126; Scott (1985), 37, 126

Selman, Robert: Selman (1971), 83, 84, 126

Shafir, M.: Shafir (1983), 81, 127

Sharedness of culture, 6, 30, 40, 59, 62–65, 68, 70, 71, 82, 91, 95, 109. See also Political culture; Public commonness

Shils, Edward: Parsons and Shils (1951), 87, 125; Parsons et al. (1961), 125

Shorter, E.: Shorter and Tilly (1974), 74, 127

Shweder, Richard: Shweder (1982), 117, 127

Sigelman, Lee: Lowery and Sigelman (1982), 82, 125

Simpson, Elizabeth Leonie: Simpson (1974), 117, 127

Sinclair, K.: Sinclair (1982), 74, 127

Smith, Tony: Smith (1985), 3, 127

Snarey, James: Snarey, Reimer, and Kohlberg (1984), 73, 74, 127

Social development. See Development, social

Sollie, Finn: Sollie (1984), 2, 127

Springer, D.: Bertilson, Springer, and Fierke (1982), 74, 121

Stone, Clarence N.: Stone (1980), 32, 82, 83, 127
Sullivan, Edmund V.: Sullivan (1977), 117, 127
Syngman Rhee, 54
Szalay, Lorand B.: Szalay and Kelly (1982), 82, 127

Thompson, E. P.: Thompson (1971), 37, 127
Tilly, Charles: Shorter and Tilly (1974), 74, 127; Tilly (1978), 37, 40, 127
Torney, Judith V.: Hess and Torney (1967), 85, 102, 124
Truth. See Validity claims, of truth
Truthfulness. See Validity claims, of truthfulness
Turiel, Elliot: Turiel (1966), 84, 127

Unitary position on conceptualization, 19–21

Vaillancourt, Pauline Marie: Vaillancourt (1986), 100, 127
Validity claims, 11, 33, 87, 109, 116; of comprehensibility, 109; of rightness, 29, 33, 41, 88, 105, 109, 110; of truth, 33, 88, 109; of truthfulness, 33, 87, 109
Van Dijk, T.: Van Dijk (1983), 74, 127
Verba, Sidney: Almond and Verba (1963), 15, 57, 58, 62, 65, 81, 82, 87, 89, 91, 92, 121; Almond and Verba (1980), 82, 121
Vygotsky, Lev: Vygotsky (1978), 117, 127

Walker, Lawrence J.: Walker (1982), 105, 127

Ward, Dana: Rosenberg, Ward, and Chilton (1988), 36, 92, 103, 126
Ways of relating and the ways of relating perspective, 1, 6–8, 26–35, 37, 40, 41, 44, 46, 47, 58, 66–72, 75, 76, 79, 80, 82, 83, 95–100, 103, 107. See also Culture; Moral relationship with others; Political culture
Weber, Max, 29, 44, 80–82; Weber (1958), 32, 54, 127
Weiner, Myron: Weiner and Huntington (1987), 2, 8, 9, 127
Weinreich, Helen: Weinreich (1977), 73, 127
Wellhofer, E. Spencer: Wellhofer (1989), 39, 66, 127
Weschler, Lawrence: Weschler (1989), 66, 127
Westernization. See Political development
White, Lynn, Jr.: White (1962), 28, 31, 32, 40, 128
Wildavsky, Aaron, 83
Williamson, Judith: Williamson (1978), 74, 128
Wilson, Amy Auerbacher: Wilson, Greenblatt, and Wilson (1981), 125, 128
Wilson, Edmund O.: Wilson (1975), 29, 128
Wilson, Richard: Wilson, Greenblatt, and Wilson (1981), 125, 128
Wolin, Sheldon: Wolin (1960), 11, 128

Yeager, F.: Yeager (1974), 74, 128

About the Book
and the Author

Stephen Chilton has argued previously that political development must be defined in terms of the moral/cognitive structures of political culture. The present work provides the philosophical and analytic framework within which that definition is embedded. This framework encompasses four major issues of social science: how we conceptualize culture; why we require a normatively grounded theory of development; how agreement over disputed concepts can be reached; and how a cross–culturally applicable conception of development can avoid moral imperialism.

Chilton systematically presents his framework and connects it with development. His analysis will be of interest to development scholars, to all social scientists concerned with the connection between normative social theory and empirical social science, and to methodologists concerned with the foundations of social theory.

STEPHEN CHILTON is assistant professor of political science at the University of Minnesota, Duluth, where he specializes in comparative politics, political psychology, and methodology. He is the author of *Defining Political Development* and (with Shawn Rosenberg and Dana Ward) *Political Reasoning and Cognition: A Piagetian View*.